CW00470374

One Hundred Years of Health-Related Social Work
1895 - 1995

Then ... Now ... Onwards

by

Joan Baraclough
Grace Dedman
Hazel Osborn
Phyllis Willmott

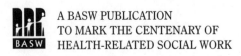

A BASW PUBLICATION
TO MARK THE CENTENARY OF
HEALTH-RELATED SOCIAL WORK

© British Association of Social Workers, 1996

All rights reserved. No part of this publication may be
reproduced, stored in a retrieval system, or
transmitted, in any form or by any means, electronic,
mechanical, photocopying, recording or otherwise,
without the prior permission of BASW Trading Limited

Published by
BASW Trading Limited
16 Kent Street
Birmingham B5 6RD

Cover design
Western Arts
0171-253 8403

British Library Cataloguing-in-Publication Data
A catalogue record for this book is available
from the British Library

ISBN 1 873878 92 3 (paperback)

Printed in Great Britain

To all patients and carers:
the reason for our being

CONTENTS

FOREWORD

Arthur Collis

One of the most rewarding of my early tasks when I became involved in cataloguing the archives of the seven organisations which came together in 1970 to form the British Association of Social Workers was to examine the extensive documentation which had been carefully preserved by the Institute of Medical Social Workers. There in black and white - often in their own handwriting - were the reports of Mary Stewart and others of the initial band of lady almoners appointed from 1895 onwards, analysing the different categories of patients with which they were dealing in the over-crowded outpatients' departments and giving their views on the problems which they faced. Then came ledgers containing the minutes of the Hospital Almoners Committee set up in 1903 to discuss the difficulties and objectives of their work and of the Hospital Almoners Council formed in 1907 to oversee the recruitment and training of almoners.

As I went through these and other volumes of minutes, journals, members' bulletins, seminar and conference reports, etc. the growth and flowering of one of the major sectors of modern social work unfolded. Here, too, was a continuing discussion of the principles underpinning social work, the practical issues involved in meeting the needs of a growing clientele in the face of changing social conditions and statutory requirements and of the consequent implications for education and training.

Files containing evidence submitted by their professional body to Royal Commissions, committees of enquiry and government working parties show how the almoners (later to be known as medical social workers) were always prepared to look beyond their own working remit and to use their personal knowledge and experience to contribute to the debate on broader problems of social welfare.

The records of the Association of Psychiatric Social Workers founded in 1929 following the introduction of specialised training in that field provide a similar source of information on the development of this sector of social work. They again show the growth of a body determined to achieve high standards of training and service. By the late 1960s both the Institute of Medical Social Workers and the Association of Psychiatric Social Workers had achieved a high level of professional status and public recognition based on the standards they set for training and practice and their registers of qualified practitioners.

When I learnt that Joan Baraclough proposed to gather together within the British Association of Social Workers a group of interested members to prepare material for a series of events to commemorate a hundred years of health-related social work I was particularly pleased to know that it was intended to produce a publication which would recount the history of this period. Those whose labours now appear in print were advised in the collation and preparation by Zofia Butrym, Lena Ashley and Brenda Holmes. The team has, I think, driven a clear, well-documented path through the wealth of material with which they were faced and although inevitably selective in some respects they provide a most interesting and valuable account of a hundred years of change and challenge. Of particular importance in light of the current position of the social work services is the way in which the earlier history leads up to an informed discussion of the impact of the wide-ranging changes which have occurred since the local authority social service departments were given responsibility for a multiplicity of services – a situation further complicated by the more recent introduction of a market style form of provision.

Some of those, including myself, who supported the generic approach to social work and argued for the unification of services and professional organisation are not entirely happy about the way events have since unfolded. I certainly would like to have seen the boundaries of social work requiring the kind of education and training provided for medical social workers and psychiatric social workers more clearly delineated to distinguish social work from ancillary welfare and caring provision.

The basic training for non-graduates entering the profession should, in my opinion, be of three years' duration, not two as at present, and more extensive provision for advanced training in the more demanding sectors of social work would help to ensure higher standards of practice as well as providing the way to a career structure for fieldworkers rising through supervisory grades to consultant level. A register of all fully trained social workers like those previously kept by IMSW and APSW and a Social Work Council responsible for the oversight of qualifications and professional performance would further guarantee standards and add to public confidence.

In congratulating those responsible for "One Hundred Years of Health-Related Social Work" I commend it not only to present and future social workers and to all those in any way involved with our personal social services but to the general public. Providing a fascinating account of the growth of a major area of social work it illuminates many of the issues which face society in seeking to meet the needs of its less fortunate members who can benefit from outside help and support.

Birmingham 1995

CONTRIBUTORS

Arthur Collis
Professor Emeritus (Social Administration), University of Birmingham. Honorary Archivist, British Association of Social Workers. One time Deputy Children's Officer, Glamorgan County Council; Chairman and Vice-President of the Association of Social Workers; ASW representative on SCOSW; signatory of BASW constitution and articles of incorporation.

Joan Baraclough
Qualified as an almoner in 1960 at University of Edinburgh. After practising at Ealing and Westminster Hospitals became Assistant General Secretary of BASW, moving to CCETSW and later to the Social Services Inspectorate of the Department of Health. A Trustee of the Social Workers Educational Trust, of the Marylebone Centre Trust and of the Welwyn Hatfield Crossroads Scheme, her main activity since retiring has been as a member of the BASW Centenary Planning Group.

Phyllis Willmott
Qualified as an almoner in 1948. After a year in practice, Mrs Willmott married and brought up her family. Later she became a researcher and lecturer in social policy at Croydon Technical College. She is the author of several books, including "The Consumer's Guide to the British Social Services" (Penguin) and "A Singular Woman: the Life of Geraldine Aves 1898-1986" (Whiting and Birch).

Grace Dedman
After a wartime job in a propeller factory's research department, Miss Dedman graduated from Manchester University in 1950 and qualified as an almoner from the Institute in 1952. She worked first at the Elizabeth Garrett Anderson Hospital and then for many years at the Royal London Hospital in a variety of posts, including Group Head. Since retirement she has been a member of the FWA Grants and Education Committees and amongst other activities is now a lay assessor for Camden Social Services Inspection Unit of Residential Homes.

Hazel Osborn (*née* Muras)
Qualified in 1954 and began work at the Royal Free Hospital, later moving to St Mary's Hospital, Paddington where she worked for several years as an almoner and as a lecturer in the medical school.

In 1971 she moved to Portsmouth as student unit supervisor for the University of Southampton. In 1974 she took up a joint appointment between the University and Hampshire Social Services Department as a Principal Officer Health and part-time lecturer. She is now a Senior Visiting Research Fellow at the University of Southampton.

Doris M. Thornton

Qualified in 1939 as an almoner and later a psychiatric social worker and held posts in a base hospital; with the Medical Research Council; as tutor with the Institute of Almoners; Group Head Almoner of the Middlesex Hospital Group for 18 years and latterly Principal Officer Health, Westminster Social Services Department. Miss Thornton was awarded a Fulbright Fellowship and spent two years in Chicago. She took an active part in both IMSW and APSW as well as in BASW and has contributed to education and training and international social work developments.

Diana Glover

Called up to serve in the armed forces in 1943, Mrs Glover became involved in welfare and after the war took the London University Extra-Mural diploma and qualified on the Institute of Almoners course in 1948. Married and worked for 20 years at Edgware General Hospital.

Jane E. Paterson

Qualified as an almoner in 1939. After working in hospitals in England and Scotland, in 1947 she was appointed to the staff of the University of Edinburgh and in 1948 began work in the General Practice Teaching Unit with Dr Scott - the first post of this kind. She wrote and spoke extensively about its value to patients and to multidisciplinary collaboration.

Ann Loxley (*née* Meunier)

Trained at the Institute of Almoners in 1958 and then worked in hospitals in Newcastle, Cardiff, Stoke Mandeville and Swindon. From 1972 to 1982 taught part time and from 1982 to 1992 full time as a Senior Lecturer at Middlesex Polytechnic on all social work qualifying courses. Her specialism was Social Work in Health Care. Founder-member and now Hon Secretary and Trustee of the Centre for Advancement of Interprofessional Education (CAIPE). For nine years a member of Enfield District Health Authority. Her husband is an engineer turned clergyman and they now have four children.

Jacquin Northcott

After graduating from the London School of Economics, trained and worked as a family caseworker. Council member of the Association of Family Caseworkers, one of the seven founding organisations of BASW. After caring for her four children she returned to work in hospitals and for the last two years has worked in a community team for elderly and physically disabled people and has obtained a Tavistock Clinic Diploma in working with the dying and the bereaved.

ACKNOWLEDGEMENTS

We wish to pay tribute to the pioneers, whose careful recording of their activities and public lectures gave us information about the origins of our profession. Our appreciation of the generality of the work and of subsequent innovators is due to the work of successive Secretaries of the Institute - Miss Edminson, Miss Roxburgh, Miss Steel and Miss Kelly; to the Directors and staff of the Institute's Training School - Miss Helen Rees and Miss Jean Snelling; to the Editors of the Journal in its various forms since 1927 and to Professor Arthur Collis, who has caringly tended the records of the predecessor organisations.

Many people have contributed to this publication, through writing, sharing reminiscences and drawing attention to archival material. We are indebted to them all.

We are especially grateful to Doris Thornton and Diana Glover for their recollections of social work during wartime; to Jane Paterson for her account of the beginning of social work in general practice; to Ann Loxley for her personal comment about training at the Institute of Almoners in 1958; and to Jacquin Northcott for her example of practice in 1995.

We thank particularly Lena Ashley, Keith Bilton, Rene Boyd, Zofia Butrym, Nora Copleston, Morag Faulds, Helena Hill, Betty Holman, Brenda Holmes, Kay McDougall, Marjorie McInnes, David N. Jones, Betty Perry, Betty Read, Janet Redfern, Kay Richards, Alice Sheridan, Betty Schwarzman and Margaret Turner for providing content and comment for this publication; and Margaret R. Richards, Diane Brown, Margaret Christelow, Jean Curry, Gillian Ingall, Kate Redlich, Chris Stanners, Rosemary Whiffen, Brenda Williams, Sylvia Woolfe and Jonathan Evans of the Royal London Hospital Archive and Museum, Lynne Amidan, archivist, Royal Free Hospital, and Clare Dunne and Lesley Hall of the Wellcome Institute for the History of Medicine.

Our very warm thanks are due to Anne and Mike Fonseka for help in preparing the text; Tracey Best, Christine Sedgwick, Lyn Nock and Sally Arkley at BASW Headquarters for help in arranging its publication.

Finally, we wish to express our appreciation to CCETSW for its support for this publication and for the centenary year as a whole.

INTRODUCTION

Joan Baraclough

The year 1995 marks the centenary of health-related social work. Changes over such a period may be enormous. Who in 1900 expected man to reach the moon in his lifetime? Changes may be temporary, suited to the needs of a particular time or they may be enduring, exemplifying core values and principles. Reflecting on the history, be it of a family, of an organisation or of a policy, while honouring the past, promotes continuity and provides a springboard to the future. The process of recording, analysing, assessing and acting can lead to new ideas and improved development.

In celebrating the centenary of health-related social work in the United Kingdom, the British Association of Social Workers (BASW) aims to encourage all social workers to recognise their heritage and to support current practitioners, managers, academics and policy makers to look forward into the twenty-first century and so further develop caring, constructive and effective ways of meeting the needs of ill people.

Throughout the country during 1995 a number of national and local events have been organised to illustrate some of the ways social workers and social service agencies, both voluntary and statutory, help people at home or in hospital to manage the impact of illness on themselves and their families.

This publication has been commissioned by BASW to provide a brief record of the development of social work in health settings between 1895 and 1995. It focuses primarily on the development of almoning, renamed medical social work in 1964, and now usually described as health-related social work.

Psychiatric social work, the other main element in health-related social work, which developed as a recognised specialism between 1930 and 1974, influenced and was influenced by the growth of medico-social work in hospitals and in the community. Its history is well documented by Jones, 1960[1]; Timms, 1964[2] and Younghusband, 1978[3]. Several of the first psychiatric social workers were almoners who went to America to train in the early thirties, thus reinforcing a trend towards international exchanges among social workers. It is interesting to speculate what the state of health-related social work today might have been if the Mental Health Course founded in 1929 at the London School of Economics and now under threat of closure had been developed as an advanced course for all social workers, rather than as a qualifying course for a particular specialism.

The publication has been designed with four chapters, each with its own principal author. The first chapter, written by Phyllis Willmott, covers the first 50 years: from the appointment of the first almoner in 1895 until the end of World War Two in 1945. When Mary Stewart took up her post at the Royal Free Hospital, London, there had been for many years considerable concern about the state of hospitals, especially in London; about overcrowding in the out-patient departments and about the abuse of free hospital facilities by those who could afford to pay. In Chapter one, Mrs Willmott describes the needs of the service users (patients) of those days and some of the ways individual workers set out to provide help. The patient, his family and the interrelationship between his illness and his social circumstances, rather than the disease, were the main focus of the almoner's attention. In order to fulfil one of their main duties, almoners carefully recorded relevant data, then analysed it and reported to management to support the case for improvements in the service. Gradually as understanding of the merits of hospital social service spread its principles were applied in municipal hospitals and to work in other services, such as child guidance and in the care of mentally ill people.

The right to intervene in other people's lives carries with it the responsibility to be well educated and well informed, as well as knowledgeable and skilful in managing human relations. From the beginning, a university education, preferably in the social sciences, and practical training at a recognised almoner training centre were seen as necessary for the development of professional knowledge and skill. By the end of World War Two, the merits of employing almoners and psychiatric social workers, especially in times of crisis, had been confirmed. Co-operation with other health professionals and with voluntary organisations in the welfare field was well established. In 1945 the Hospital Almoners Association and the Institute of Hospital Almoners combined to form the Institute of Almoners, and with the Association of Psychiatric Social Workers, which also became a company limited by guarantee that year, formed a small but sound professional base from which social work in the NHS has developed.

In writing this chapter, Mrs Willmott has drawn heavily on the content of the Golden Jubilee Number of the Almoner, published in November 1953 to mark the 50th anniversary of the formation of the professional association. The essays by Miss L. C. Marx, Miss M. W. Edminson and Miss M. J. Roxburgh contain personal recollections of their (and therefore our) predecessors, including some of the few who remembered work in the years before 1914. Doris Thornton and

Diana Glover in Vignettes 1 and 2 portray vividly their personal experiences of hospital social work in World War Two. Thus we have a living and recorded history. It is striking that many of the values and principles on which social work is based today were in place from the beginning.

Chapter Two deals with the years 1946-1973. Grace Dedman describes the key features of a period which encompassed both the introduction and the reorganisation of the National Health Service and many changes in the Welfare State. Through their professional associations and their journals, members of the Institute of Almoners and of the Association of Psychiatric Social Workers continued their practice of commenting on social policy issues.

With the implementation of the National Health Service Act 1946 on 5 July 1948 health care for all was provided free at the point of use and at a stroke changed the nature of the hospital social workers' task. They no longer had a duty to assess what patients should pay for their medical care. They could concentrate on practising "proper social work", helping people to regain their independence and accommodate the consequences of illness and disability. The implementation of the National Assistance Act 1948 finally abolished the Poor Law, though not those who were aged, sick, poor or needy.

There were a burgeoning and sharing of ideas about the nature of social work practice and the content of professional education in social work circles and with doctors and other professional and lay people at home and with social work colleagues in other countries.

In the first decade of the NHS the shortage of sufficient numbers of well-qualified staff to meet the growing demand for services led to many innovations in practice, in the organisation of hospital social work departments and in education and training. The number of almoners and psychiatric social workers increased; most new posts were in hospitals, and gradually in local authority health and welfare departments. The first almoner to work with a group of general practitioners was Jane Paterson, who took up her post in what became the General Practice Teaching Unit of Edinburgh University in 1947. Her account of that development is given in Vignette 3. The Institute's efforts to increase the supply of trained almoners took the form of a "great experiment" in which five Emergency (specially designed shorter qualifying) Courses between 1946 and 1949 trained 272 almoners, an addition to the workforce of almost 25%.

The contribution of women during two world wars had changed attitudes. Women seeking to work or to return to work were no longer discouraged from doing so, though married women with young children had more difficulty. The Association of Part-time Social Workers formed in 1959 pressed for greater provision for part-time social workers and urged the universities and professional bodies to provide courses for married women seeking to return to work. The NHS was to be well served by locum and part-time social workers.

Miss Dedman recalls the struggles for recognition as an independent profession. Registration was a major issue for many health professionals in the early years of the NHS. Both the Institute of Almoners and the Association of Psychiatric Social Workers had approved courses of qualifying training and maintained registers of qualified staff from the earliest days. In 1951, a government committee chaired by Sir Zachary Cope proposed statutory registration for health professionals as medical auxiliaries. Almoners, together with occupational therapists and speech therapists on the committee, wrote a minority report rejecting the proposal on the grounds that it would "deny to any profession full responsibility for maintaining its own standards of qualification, of ethics and of practice . . .". "The word 'auxiliary' has by common use come to denote an untrained or partially trained person."

Though psychiatric social workers did not come within the remit of the Cope Committee, similar questions were raised in the deliberations of the Mackintosh Committee. The stand taken marked a watershed for the profession. The current debates about the establishment of a General Social Services Council carry many echoes of these reports.

Though often portrayed as the handmaidens of doctors, almoners in the fifties saw themselves as members of a multidisciplinary team, contributing not only to patient care but to the education and training of medical students, nurses and others. It was a very useful way to promote interprofessional understanding and trust.

For many social workers today, the fifties and sixties represented a golden age when they were part of a widely acclaimed and innovative public service: when they belonged to a specialist professional association that called for high standards in practice and education and which provided a network of professional fellowship and support to last a lifetime. And yet they recognised the need for change, though not all welcomed the prospect. Change was needed to deal with more of the social problems in the community; to benefit from advances in medicine and from the introduction of new technology.

Increasingly, almoners and psychiatric social workers regarded themselves as part of the wider world of social work. Almoners marked their identification with the larger whole in 1964, when the Institute changed its name and became the Institute of Medical Social Workers. From 1962, both the Institute and the Association of Psychiatric Social Workers were key players in the Standing Conference of Organisations of Social Workers as it worked to establish a unified professional body. That the British Association of Social Workers came into being in the midst of major changes in the structure and organisation of the social services and as all responsibility for training was about to be vested in one central body, prompts some interesting questions about the availability, energy and distribution of tasks among active members of the profession. Was too much attempted in too short a time? What would have been different if the remits of the Kilbrandon and Seebohm Committees had allowed them to consider the future of social work in the Health Service? Would the transfer of medical social workers and psychiatric social workers from the employment by the NHS have become such an issue had BASW been firmly established sooner and the Central Council for Education and Training in Social Work (CCETSW) had supported the need for specialist training?

Social policy issues featured strongly on the national political agenda in the late sixties and early seventies. Social workers were active and articulate in commenting on the emerging proposals for the reorganisation of the social work services in Scotland and social services in England and Wales; for the reorganisation of the National Health Service and of local government. They shared their expertise about the needs of patients and were proactive in support of the kind of services they thought would meet needs. The fact that there were differences in the content and timing of the introduction of the relevant legislation in each of the home countries was both a strength and a weakness as far as health-related social workers were concerned. Would social workers in the health field have felt less marginalised if they had joined the social services departments from their inception? What impact did the changes have on patients and on the provision of services?

Before leaving this period, it is important to pay tribute to the many members of other professions and lay people who took part in the development of medical and psychiatric social work and to the work of the professional bodies. Over the years, until 1968, many eminent men served as Chairman or Honorary Treasurer of the Institute of Medical Social Workers. Almoners certainly benefited from having a multidisciplinary council, as did psychiatric social workers.

Chapter Three, written by Hazel Osborn, perhaps better known to some generations of social workers and doctors as Hazel Muras, covers the period from 1974 to the present day. She examines the major changes in a period when medical and psychiatric social workers became part of a holistic approach to social service provision. Health-based social workers were clearly social workers first and specialists second, though some would say, rather, local government officers first and social workers second.

Mrs Osborn describes the efforts made by social workers transferred from the NHS to become assimilated in the local authority departments at a time when both the NHS and local government were in the throes of reorganisation. She draws attention to the extensive changes in attitudes to welfare as increasing unemployment and a growing number of very old, frail people led to financial constraints and the introduction of a mixed economy of care during the 1980s.

She points out too that attitudes to the rights of individuals were changing. Anti-discrimination and data protection legislation was reinforcing many social work values. Many of the principles about confidentiality contained in the Institute of Almoners statement of 1947 are reiterated in guidance on access to personal files. Patients became consumers and then service users, with charters which set out their rights and gave assurances about the quality of service.

The Children Act 1989 and the NHS and Community Care Act 1990 have brought fundamental changes in social work practice. Partnerships with parents, parental responsibility; partnership with users and carers, assessment of need and care management are the current cornerstones. The language is new; the organisational arrangements of the services are different, but the underlying values seem the same.

In Chapter Four Joan Baraclough speculates on the future and considers some of the issues to be faced by health-related social workers today and in the years leading to and beyond the millennium. Increasing enpowerment of service users; continuing struggles to fund services; improved interprofessional collaboration; increased skill mix in patient care teams; loosening of professional boundaries; tightening of professional standards: these are some of the targets for the future. History suggests that by listening to the patient – relating together his health and social needs, capacities and resources in a positive professional environment, – greatest progress may be made.

In the past 25 years, social work has been scrutinised as never before. Public enquiries and extensive media coverage when things go wrong have become commonplace. Internal inspection units and government inspectors sometimes can redress the balance by highlighting the positives as well as the negatives, while professional associations have a crucial role to play in adhering to values and principles, setting standards and providing professional refreshment and support at all times, not only when trouble arrives. Social workers and their employers have to work at communication skills: with users and their families and carers; with fellow professionals; with politicians; with the media and with the general public, if there is to be greater knowledge and understanding of the aims and objectives of social work.

As a profession, social work would do well to reassess and restate its core values and to re-examine and revitalise professional education for work with sick people, whether they are in hospital or at home, in view of the very high proportion referred to social service agencies when their problems have in fact a health component. Systems of staff support and self-regulation need to be strengthened, in the light of current social problems and changing ethical attitudes. Not least there is a need to create a climate of public awareness and trust in quality services.

Such objectives will not be easy to achieve against a background of continuing struggles to fund services. Yet are they more demanding than the tasks of the pioneers who started with the aim of helping patients to obtain full and proper benefit from the medical and nursing skills provided by hospitals? One hundred years ago society was concerned at the abuse of hospitals. Today, as a society and as social workers, we are appalled at the abuse of individuals. Problems of ill health, disability, poverty and poor housing remain. Increased public understanding of the nature of need and of the social work contribution helps to generate a more positive climate in which to tackle social problems.

As social workers we are obliged to persevere, despite stress-related illness or even physical assault. We shall continue to do so, with commitment, courage and compassion, enriched through sound continuing professional education and professional and public support.

In some measure, by outlining its history and by celebrating the continuity and change in 100 years of health-related social work, we hope we have made a contribution to that end.

References

[1] Jones, K., Mental Health and Social Policy 1845-1959, Routledge and Kegan Paul, 1960

[2] Timms, N., Psychiatric Social Work in Great Britain (1939-1962), Routledge and Kegan Paul, 1964

[3] Younghusband, E.L., Social Work in Britain 1950-1975 (2 volumes), George Allen & Unwin, 1978

CHAPTER ONE

1895-1945: THE FIRST 50 YEARS

Phyllis Willmott

Social work with and for the sick and disabled people has a long history which began 100 years ago with the appointment of the first almoner in 1895 to the Royal Free Hospital then in Gray's Inn Road, London. Miss Mary Stewart, formerly secretary of the St Pancras office of the Charity Organisation Society (COS), was to become the founding figure of a new profession. She owed her appointment to the reforming zeal and determination of Sir Charles Loch, the renowned Secretary of the COS. Firm advocate of planned and constructive charitable aid, he sought to end what he and others at the time believed to be the abuse of the out-patient departments of the voluntary hospitals that had led them to becoming "scandalously overcrowded".

One reason for the overcrowding was that, apart from private medical care and the limited provisions under the Poor Law, there was nowhere else for people to go for free treatment. By 1891, public concern about the pressure on hospitals had led to the setting up of a Select Committee of the House of Lords. Sir Charles proposed to the committee that trained social workers within hospitals were needed to prevent the "abuse" of the out-patient department by patients thought to be in a position to pay for their treatment or to be so poor as to be unable to benefit from it.

In one of her monthly reports to the Hospital Board soon after she began work at the Royal Free (with a salary of £100 a year paid for by the Charity Organisation Society) Miss Stewart identified three groups of patients. There were those who were in (or could be expected to join) a provident medical association; those unable to do so; and those needing food and other material help from private charity or the Poor Law. She was to discover before long that pressing those she saw to join a provident association or friendly society was not very successful. Of the 350 patients she referred to such bodies over a period of five months in 1897 only 17 were known to have joined.

It was an irony that although her appointment had been made with the main purpose of checking out-patient abuse, Miss Stewart's first two years proved difficult partly because the medical and surgical staff objected to the new system. They protested that it tended to limit the number of out-patients and so "militate against the excellence of teaching material". Many of the almoners appointed at other hospitals in the following years found that at first medical/nursing staff or administrative members of the hospital staff regarded them with some suspicion. It was for this reason that at St Thomas's in the early years almoners were instructed to walk outside instead of along the corridors so as "not to be noticed" by medical and nursing staff. They also had to be careful about their appearance:

> Long skirts were in fashion, but trains were not allowed and any assistant coming to St. Thomas's on a Saturday morning dressed to play hockey later was sent home because her skirt was four inches off the ground - the regulation length for hockey. White coats did not appear for some time, but the large hats of the period were worn. [1]

The latter part of the nineteenth century was the period in which Charles Booth was carrying out his great survey of London and discovering the extent of unavoidable poverty.

It was also the time that the COS (to become the Family Welfare Association in 1946) still believed encouraging thrift was the way to help the poor, not the uncontrolled charitable giving that was thought to encourage dependency. Trained as they were by the COS it was not surprising that the first almoner, and others who followed in the early years of the twentieth century, began with a stronger belief in the virtues of thrift and self-help than the conditions of the time proved to warrant. But face to face in those overcrowded out-patient departments with the unavoidable hardship that ill health could bring, the early almoners were soon to become aware of the harsh lives of those they saw, and of their wider needs, as their reports made clear.

> **An Early Case of Hardship.** MN, a labourer aged 52, wife, and three children, all dependent. Attends casualty for dressing for a poisoned finger three times a day. Rent 5s. 6d - three weeks owing. Wife earning 6s. a week now and again by step cleaning etc. [Poor Law] Guardians giving six loaves. (Miss Stewart's report, Royal Free Hospital, 1896.)

> **Aiming to meet wider needs** - To ensure as far as possible that all outpatients to whom treatment is granted shall benefit to the full by that treatment, and that no time or money shall be withheld either by the patient or by charitable agencies to enable the patient to co-operate with the hospital in carrying out the prescribed

treatment. (Miss Cummins's second report, St Thomas's Hospital, 1906.)

Queen Victoria's death in 1901 marked the end of an era. In 1908 the Old Age Pensions Act introduced pensions of 1s (5p) to 5s (25p) a week for those over 70 years of age, subject to a means test, but no longer to the stigma of the Poor Law. [2] Three years later came the National Insurance Act 1911. It gave insured workers the right to sickness benefits, treatment from a "panel" doctor in time of sickness, care in sanatoriums if suffering tuberculosis; but no hospital treatment nor any health care for other members of the insured workers' families. However, the Act signified the development of a new spirit with its preamble that it was *"an Act to provide for insurance against loss of health and for the prevention and cure of sickness"*.

Although during these years the number of hospital almoners was only slowly increasing, in 1910 Miss Mudd - a "lady of independent means" who had first worked in London at St George's Hospital - became the first almoner appointed to a provinicial teaching hospital outside London. She could perhaps also lay claim to have been the first group almoner as, with one assistant and one student, she served three hospitals: the Leeds General Infirmary, the Public Dispensary, and the Women's Children's Hospital. Her task could not have been an easy one:

Housing conditions were deplorable. The majority were back-to-back type. Milk as an article of diet was rare, the common food for babies was "pobs", bread soaked in water, with the result that rickets, described by Miss Mudd as "the scourge of the working population", was universal and straight legs in adults almost unknown. Children seldom walked until they were three or four years old and a common sight in the back streets was races between children of up to four or five on their bare behinds - knickers were not worn. [3]

In 1903, eight years after the pioneering appointment of Miss Stewart, the Hospital Almoners' Committee was set up. It had eight members who were almoners, three COS staff and two voluntary visitors. The committee met monthly and at one of its first meetings set out "the aims of the almoners work". Sandwiched between the two original aims of "reducing the number of casualty patients" and "encouraging thrift" was an important third: "To interview patients to discover if the doctor's advice can be satisfactorily followed."

Four years later (1907), the Hospital Almoners' Council was founded (not to be confused with the Committee, which continued to exist). The council took over responsibility for training, and from then on the role of the COS gradually diminished. This period also marked the beginning of an interest in American practice, particularly in the work of Dr Richard Cabot of Boston, Massachusetts, who was felt to express "all that almoners were striving for, and the ideals of medical social service".

As it had from the time of Miss Mary Stewart's move from the St Pancras office of COS to the Royal Free Hospital, training continued to be based on several months' work, first in a COS office and then in a hospital. This was supplemented by attendance at lectures at the School of Sociology (until its amalgamation in 1912 with the London School of Economics). Certificates were awarded to successful candidates (one for "full" and one for "assistant" almoners) and about half of all applicants for training were being refused by 1913.

Changes brought by the First World War: 1914-1918

As one of the most eminent commentators on social welfare was to later point out, the very destructiveness of wars demands "the organisation of services to repair and heal".[4] The First World War was the impetus that led to a scheme for the diagnosis and treatment of venereal disease, spurred on the movement for the care of mothers and young children and later (in 1919) to the creation of the Ministry of Health. Coupled with earlier changes, such as those for Public Health and National Insurance, the outbreak of the Great War led to growing awareness of the value of the services that almoners could offer. As the Hospital Almoners' Council put it in its annual report at the time, hospitals were "increasingly alive to the importance of after-care and of newer developments such as ante-natal, post-natal and temperance work". It marked a change expressed at the same time by the Council in its revision of the "duties" (which we would now call functions) of almoners.

1. To check the abuse of the out-patient department by patients in a position to pay for treatment, or insured under the National Insurance Act and entitled to the services of a panel doctor and not needing special hospital treatment, or those too poor to benefit by any assistance other than that obtainable through the Poor Law.

2. To ensure that all out-patients shall benefit to the full by treatment by securing, with the assistance of outside charitable agencies, the full co-operation of patient in carrying out treatment.

3. To act as a connecting link between the out-patient department and outside charities. [5]

With the almost immediate influx of large numbers of wounded men, almoners were soon faced with the need for both material and personal help for the men and their relatives at the same time as other work was expanding. For example, by this time Miss Cummins (in 1905 the first almoner appointed at St Thomas's Hospital) was "yearning" to expand the work with out-patients to include in-patients "whose personal problems so often and so fatally retarded their progress to health".

In 1909 interested members of St Thomas's Hospital staff and their supporters had been persuaded by Miss Cummins to set up the Northcote Trust to develop an after-care service for mothers and their babies in a small house opposite the hospital where clinics, classes and advice were available. This was successful enough to be commended in the Local Government Board's report on infant mortality in 1915 - and despite Miss Cummins's own cautious comment in her annual report at the time:

"It is difficult to press for one and a half pints of milk a day to be taken for the baby and the two year old when the family of six have an income of 24s. [£1.20p] and rent is 7s. [35p]".

The Northcote Trust also enabled St Thomas's almoners to promote social care of tuberculous patients at a time when this disease was a national scourge. This pioneer work carried on until, in 1919, the treatment and care of those suffering from tuberculosis became a statutory responsibility carried out at dispensaries and clinics everywhere.

Throughout the war the Hospital Almoners' Council continued to promote and emphasise the importance of having "an experienced social worker for dealing with those cases where satisfactory work cannot be done without radical changes in the homes conditions of the patient". By 1919 (almost 25 years after the appointment of Mary Stewart) the number of almoners in hospitals had reached 46. As hospitals in other parts of the country recruited almoners to their staff, the Hospital Almoners' Council successfully organised arrangements for centres where student almoners could take part of their training outside London.

After the war

The numbers of students continued to increase (albeit slowly) after the war ended. Interest in the work of the Council amongst members rose too. In 1922 the Council had become the Institute of Hospital Almoners. The committee of members had already become the Hospital Almoners' Association and was urging its qualified members to use the letters AIHA after their names. A little earlier (1919) the Ministry of Health had been created (with responsibility for health, housing, sanitation, treatment of epidemics and sewage); its predecessor the Local Government Board had been abolished.

Although the Unemployment Insurance Act of 1920 provided partial protection, the economic conditions that followed the end of the war and high unemployment brought much hardship and misery. The voluntary hospitals were amongst those affected by the economic difficulties, and in the year that the Hospitals Almoners' Association was formally constituted an extraordinary meeting was called to discuss what part, if any, almoners should play if patients had to be asked to pay for treatment.

Three years later the Council minuted a conviction that "a hospital is able to collect payments more efficiently and fairly, and to produce more willing contributions to its revenue by the employment of a trained almoner than by any other means". Subsequently the constraints this approach imposed on the social work role were recognised and concern grew to find "the best method of making the public realise that an almoner should not be primarily appointed to collect money, but to do social work". It was an issue that was to exercise the profession for the next 20 years.

Although a series of crashes on the New York stock exchange in 1928 brought a world economic crisis, for social work at this time there were signs of a new growth. In 1928 the first international conference of social workers was held in Paris. A representative from the Institute reported that she had gained "a clearer realisation of the universal nature of social problems and of a growing social conscience and a desire to solve them". Social studies departments of universities in all parts of Britain were co-operating with the Council on training schemes. Another new development with which it was connected was that of the child guidance movement in which the Commonwealth Fund of America played a part, and subsequently the Maudsley Hospital. In 1929 the first mental health course began at the London School of Economics, headed by Sibyl Clement Brown who had qualified under the Commonwealth Fund scheme to become the first British psychiatric social worker. Although not an almoner, Miss Clement Brown was closely associated with the profession and many of those who followed in her pioneering footsteps began their careers in hospital social work. There were continuing close ties from then on between psychiatric and medico-social workers. The Association of Psychiatric Social Workers was formed in 1930.

Years of depression

In 1931 unemployment was approaching 3,000,000. Many unemployed men left their homes and were wandering the country in search of work, and many from this pool of "homeless poor" were still forced to seek help under the Poor Law, especially when health broke down. For almoners, however, these grim years were a time of a move to new openings for work.

This came about in 1929 when the Local Government Act abolished the hated Boards of Guardians, and transferred responsibility for Poor Law infirmaries to local authorities. Under the new arrangements the way was opened to promote the employment of trained almoners in the municipal hospitals. It was an opportunity quickly seized.

The county of Surrey was the first to appoint a trained almoner to its staff at the Kingston Hospital. In some areas almoners were responsible to the Medical Superintendent, in others to the chief officer of Public Assistance. In local authority hospitals under the new legislation treatment was still subject to assessment so that almoners' work continued to be concerned with what patients must or could pay for their treatment as well as helping with personal and material needs. In hospitals where every inpatient had to be interviewed it is not surprising if often "casework was buried deep under the load of routine duties". [6]

By the early 1930s the London County Council (LCC) had begun to appoint almoners, and by 1935 it was planning to extend this service to all of its 28 municipal hospitals. Enid Warren (who, almost 40 years later, was to become the first chairman of BASW) was one of those who took up the challenge. Qualifying as an almoner in 1926, she moved that year from a small voluntary hospital in Greenwich (the Miller General) to become the first almoner at Archway Hospital which is now part of the much larger Whittington Hospital. As she described it near the end of her life:

It was a nice little hospital, just through the park [from where she lived] . . . a single-handed hospital, although they had something like 600 beds. It was a hospital with a very nice atmosphere, and I had my own office which, in fact, was a four-bedded ward. This was my first experience of being in charge of a department. [7]

Although numbers were still small compared with those in professional social work today, a record total of new posts was being advertised at this time. These included not only posts in the United Kingdom but also abroad. Almoners were by 1935 to be found in Paris, Stockholm, Melbourne, Sydney and Perth. Links with Australia had been forged and in 1929 Miss Agnes MacIntyre left London to inaugurate medical social work at Melbourne Hospital. This was the beginning not only of a connection between the Institute of Almoners and Australia but also of British influence in the establishment of basic social work training there.

In 1933 Miss Helen Rees succeeded Miss MacIntyre at Melbourne, later moved to Sydney, and remained there until 1941. During these years an Institute of Almoners for New South Wales was established and in 1937 this affiliated with what can justly be claimed to have been its parent body in London.

In the preceding pages the assessment of what patients could afford to contribute to the costs of treatment at a time when free treatment was rarely available and the part almoners played in this loomed large. What has not so far been mentioned is the almoners' work in enabling patients to meet the expenses of illness. Even where hospital treatment was free (as, for example, it was for those able to secure a "subscriber's letter" in the case of the voluntary hospitals) there were often other expenses it was hard for the patient to meet. In whole or in part, dentures, spectacles, surgical appliances, artificial limbs and wheelchairs had to be paid for, along with convalescence treatment, long-term medication such as insulin for diabetics, and extra nourishment so often prescribed (but not provided for) by medical prescription.

Fortunately, from a mix of training and experience, almoners invariably developed an extensive knowledge of national and local charitable sources from which they could obtain money for their patients' special needs. An important – and time-consuming – part of the almoner's work from the earliest years was therefore devoted to applying to benevolent societies, trade guilds and charities, or to hospital subscribers, for "surgical aid letters".

Recognition of the benefits of this work to the patients' recovery led many an almoner to make the case for clerical help to deal with the additional correspondence this entailed. When all else failed, Samaritan or other funds within the hospital were also a source of funds to which almoners could turn - and indeed were sometimes asked to administer.

The Second World War

The outbreak of the Second World War in September 1939 marked the end of an uneasy period overshadowed by the rise to power of Hitler and the growing threat of German militarism. For some time before the war began both the Council of the Institute and the Hospital Almoners' Association, as well as many individual almoners, were doing what they could to help over the plight of refugees from central Europe.

What was far more difficult was to decide on a plan of action for the Institute and its members if war came, and for some days when it did there was no clear picture of what the almoner's role in war-time would be. The Council had decided in July that training would stop, and in September moved its office to Oxford. In the hospitals some almoners were actually informed that they were no longer required, whereas others were offered living quarters so that they could be there in an emergency. By Christmas, the wartime Emergency Medical Service had sent out a circular advising hospitals to keep their almoners. The Ministry of Labour had classified almoning amongst the "reserved occupations". The Institute and its staff under General Secretary Miss M. J. Roxburgh had moved back to London and arrangements for training of students continued but under Miss A. B. Read, newly appointed as full-time tutor.

Despite the disruptions and many acute problems caused by the war, in 1941 (thanks partly to a gift from Australian almoners) another initiative was being planned. It was that research should be carried out to find out what almoners were doing throughout the country. The Council appointed Miss Helen Rees for this new venture. She returned from Australia to take up her new post after a perilous wartime sea journey across the world.

In the same year the Hospital Almoners' Association was asked to prepare evidence for the Beveridge Committee (set up in 1941 to survey the existing schemes of social insurance and allied services). The following year the Association was invited by the Royal College of Physicians to prepare a memorandum on the contribution almoners could make to teaching social medicine to medical students. And in 1943 the Institute of Hospital Almoners (because of its responsibility for training) was negotiating with the Ministry of Health on the recruitment of suitable almoner students and the maintaining of suitable standards.

Another important and related change took place in 1945 when the two bodies serving almoners (the IHA and the HAA) amalgamated into one body to be known as the Institute of Almoners. The new title reflected the fact that after the war almoners were working in agencies other than hospitals; in clinics and in voluntary organisations; and that training and practice were two sides of the same coin.

The war had brought a new appreciation of the contribution almoning and psychiatric social work could make to ease problems caused by the disruptions to normal life. First the evacuation programme and later the Blitz inflicted acute stresses on many people and families.

In 1940 a Ministry of Health circular asked that almoners should be employed at all hospitals where large numbers of emergency patients were being admitted and, furthermore, should be concerned not only with the assessment of means but with "the whole range of services which a trained or experienced almoner renders towards the social welfare and after-care of the patient". [9]

A Chief Welfare Officer (Miss Geraldine Aves) was appointed by the Ministry of Health to help deal with the social problems arising from evacuation – by recruiting social workers (often almoners) as regional welfare officers.[10] When the devastating effects of the Blitz followed, a Special Commissioner, Henry Willink, was appointed to co-ordinate services for homeless people in London.[11] He also quickly decided that what was needed was "experienced social workers" (who became known for a time as "Mr Willink's young ladies").

In London, almoners took their part with other social workers who rallied to help in the confusion resulting from the first serious air-raids. Some of these remained on the staff of the Commissioner, working in shelters and rest-centres. Others went back to their hospital posts when the first shock of the blitz was over. [12]

"Although as Mr Willink's young ladies (a satirical title, by the way, not intended to flatter) we didn't do social work as such, it seems to me that what we did do was to try (and sometimes succeed) to influence attitudes among local authority officers - and quite often the WVS - towards homeless people in trouble. The

Poor Law set up was not involved with the London homeless, but one constantly met with the Poor Law attitudes among those who ran the rest-centres". [13]

Other vivid accounts of social work in hospitals during the war are given in Vignettes 1 and 2.

As Titmuss pointed out in his monumental social history of the war, "trained and experienced social workers had generally been ignored by Government departments" until 1940, when "the situation changed completely" to one in which the "value of trained staff, from almoners in hospitals and clinics to social workers engaged on psychiatric work, child care and family case-work, rose in official esteem". [14]

In 1919, 25 years after Miss Mary Stewart began working with outpatients in a voluntary hospital as the first trained hospital almoner, the numbers of almoners had reached only 46. Another 25 years on that number had increased more than tenfold but many more were needed, especially in voluntary and public hospitals outside London; in clinics and increasingly in community settings. Although still a small profession in 1945, thanks to the commitment and determination of its pioneer members, the professional bodies they created and their successors, medical social work could claim to be firmly established, but there were still many challenges waiting to be faced in the years ahead.

References

[1] The Almoner, Golden Jubilee Edition, November 1953

[2] P. Gregg, A Social and Economic History of Britain, 1760-1965, Harrap, 1965 Edition

[3] The Almoner, ibid

[4] R. Titmuss, Problems of Social Policy, History of the Second World War, HMSO, 1950

[5] Annual Report, Hospital Almoners' Council, 1914

[6] The Almoner, ibid

[7] Portrait of a Social Worker, Enid C. Warren OBE, 1903-1980. A tribute from colleagues and friends, BASW, 1982

[8] The Almoner, ibid

[9] Circular 2232, Ministry of Health, 1940

[10] P. M. Willmott, A Singular Woman, The Life of Geraldine Aves 1898-1986, Whiting & Birch, 1992

[11] Willink was one of three Special Commissioners appointed for the problems brought by the Blitz. See Titmuss, ibid

[12] The Almoner, ibid

[13] E. Hope Murrray, personal communication, 1994

[14] R. Titmuss, ibid

Patients in the Out-patient Department of the London Hospital, circa *1912*

The Royal Free Hospital, Gray's Inn Road, London

St George's Hospital, Hyde Park Corner, London

Westminster Hospital, Broad Walk, London

St Thomas's Hospital, Lambeth

Mary Stewart, appointed to
Royal Free Hospital, 1895

Edith Mudd, appointed to St George's Hospital, 1898 and in 1910
opened department at Leeds General Infirmary

Anne Cummins, appointed St Thomas's Hospital, 1905

Agnes MacIntyre, first almoner in Australia:
appointed to the Royal Melbourne Hospital, 1929

Listening to a young mother's worries about her child, 1952

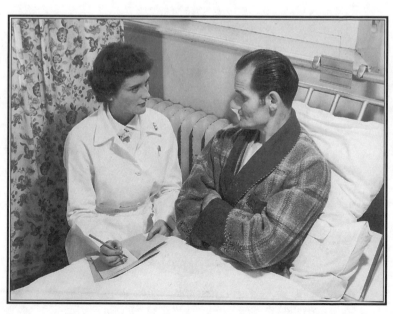

Exploring the consequences of being in hospital, 1950s

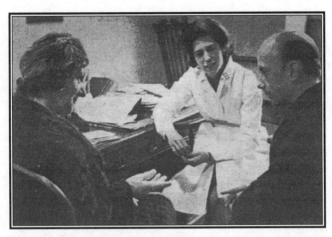

Illness brings new problems, not only to patients but to their families, who may have many anxieties over their care. The radiotherapy almoner often sees the relatives of patients attending for treatment and discusses with them the many ways in which help can be provided. It is helpful to them to feel that they can look to the hospital for advice and support both during and after treatment, 1964.

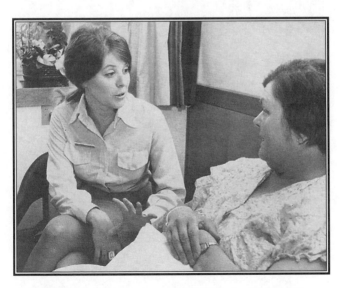

Exploring the consequences of being in hospital, 1969

TEAMWORK

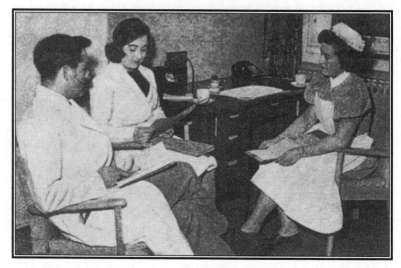

A ward team at work, 1963

Hospital Resettlement Conference, patient, doctor, DRO and medical social worker, 1965

CHAPTER TWO

1946-1973:
RECONSTRUCTION AND INTEGRATION:
SOCIAL WORK IN
THE NATIONAL HEALTH SERVICE

Grace Dedman

The period from 1946 to 1973 was a very significant and stimulating time for health-related social work. After the constraints of war, social work was free once again to develop, to enjoy professional exchanges across the world and, most important, to practise in a fundamentally changed social context.

Planning for national reconstruction took place even while war was being waged, so strong was the determination to overcome the bitter memories of the thirties depression, and to ensure that after the war everyone should enjoy a better level of personal and social security. Interest in social and preventive medicine and in psychological medicine was growing, driven to some extent by concern for the plight of civilian casualties, evacuees, refugees and returning service personnel. All professions were reviewing their roles. It was a time of hope and new beginnings.

A whole portfolio of new legislation finally abolished the Poor Law and laid the foundations of the Welfare State. The Education Act 1944, the Disabled Persons (Employment) Act 1944, the Family Allowances Act 1945, the National Insurance Act 1946, the Children's Act 1948 and the National Assistance Act 1948 were the means by which Beveridge's pre-war monstrosities of Want, Disease, Ignorance, Squalor and Idleness were to be defeated.

The most important change for almoners and psychiatric social workers was the introduction of the National Health Service. The National Health Service Act of 1946 came into force on 5 July 1948. The new service was available to people of all ages, across the whole social spectrum, and was free at the point of use. It was organised in three parts:

1. Hospital and Specialist Services which it was the duty of the Minister of Health to provide.
2. Health Services provided by Local Health Authorities.
3. General Medical and Dental Services, Pharmaceutical and supplementary Ophthalmic Services managed through Executive Councils.

Illness was defined to include mental disorders and any disability and injury requiring medical or dental treatment or nursing.

Almoners and psychiatric social workers in the hospital service were employed by Hospital Management Committees and Boards of Governors. They were not under the management of doctors or matrons, and were expected to exercise independent professional judgement, and did. They ran their own departments, in many cases known as Social Service Departments rather than Almoners Departments – certainly a more appropriate term in those hospitals (usually large teaching hospitals) with psychiatric units and psychiatric social workers who were part of a unified department, managed by a Head Almoner.

One of the recommendations of the Royal College of Physicians' 1943 Report on Social and Preventive Medicine had urged "all hospitals should employ properly trained almoners and psychiatric social workers, both in the case of patients and in teaching medical students".[1]

The first decade after the introduction of the NHS was later described as "a time of experiment and development of the services in many directions", while the second decade was seen as "surely proving the need not only for consolidation and further experiment, but also for serious and urgent study of the problems of communication and co-ordination between the various services and workers concerned with health and welfare in all its branches".[2]

The period was certainly one in which there were major changes to the nature of the almoner's role and to that of psychiatric social workers. There was a flowering of social work practice as it integrated psychoanalytic thinking. Emphasis on the value of work in the community was growing. People being referred to almoners and psychiatric social workers came from every walk of life. That illness could bring social, emotional and practical problems to anyone was well recognised. What was much less in evidence was professional and public knowledge and understanding of what working with social workers could achieve.

The social work task in the NHS

From the earliest days, almoners and then psychiatric social workers have struggled to define the nature of their task and to gain acceptance of what they saw as its essential elements.

Casework was the main method of practice until well into the 1960s, though community social work, group work and family therapy were beginning to make their mark generally. Miss E.H.

Davison's definition of casework in 1965 is useful in conveying what was understood by this term at that date. *"Social casework is a personal service, provided by qualified workers for those who require skilled help in resolving some personal or family problem. Its aim is to relieve stress, both material and emotional, and to help the client to achieve a realistic adjustment to his social circumstances and mutual satisfaction in his personal relationships.*

The caseworker seeks to do this by means of a careful study of the client in his family and social setting, and of his problem: by the establishment of a co-operative relationship with him, in which his own capacity for dealing with his problem is increased, and by the mobilisation of such other resources or professional aid as might be appropriate."[3]

In contrast, the General Secretary of the Institute of Almoners, Miss A.D. Kelly, wrote in 1961 of an experience in 1935 when *"in a quasi-administrative, quasi-social work capacity I saw 100 new casualty patients in the course of a day. This was exceptional, but many of the older generation must remember the constant and speedy interviews accompanied by rapid notes of relevant factors which somehow serve both administrative and social purposes. . . . It is a tribute to the older generation that they did do extremely valuable social work, despite administrative pressures".*[4]

To us today that struggle to work with ever-present financial and administrative tasks, whilst also offering help with the complexity of social and emotional problems, has a familiar ring. In 1948 it was thought it had been largely resolved.

The Minister of Health, Aneurin Bevan, in a speech to the Annual General Meeting of the Institute of Almoners in March 1948 forecast how the introduction of the National Health Service would change the almoner's task. He said: *"At once a barrier will be lifted between the almoner and the patient and it will be possible for the almoner to approach the patient quite independently of financial considerations. . . . It is not possible to treat a patient irrespective of the social context in which the patient lives. . . . The almoner has become a very important part indeed of modern healing work . . . is going to be a very important link between the different sections of the Health Service."*

He also pointed out that an almoner would *"have to go out rather more and cover a much wider district, but she will also have available to her much wider facilities".*[5]

In September 1948 the Ministry of Health issued a Memorandum emphasising the point that the almoner's place in the NHS was that of medical social worker and that *"their work should be confined to tasks for which they have special qualifications".*

Duties of the medical social worker

1. Social investigation and interviews to provide understanding of the social background of the patient and in particular to give the doctor information which is relevant to diagnosis and treatment.
2. Social action to minimise personal anxieties, family difficulties and other problems during illness.
3. Making of arrangements with the Local Health Authorities for the home visiting of patients who may for a time or, in some instances, for a long period, need help to ensure that the value of their treatment is not lost.

Ministry of Health: HMC (48) 53/BG (48) 57. 1946. [6]

The Institute of Almoners welcomed the circular, but pointed out that the decision as to who should do the home visit should rest with the almoner, according to the needs of the patient. Without the constraints of financial assessment and with the prospect of widening opportunities the future looked bright. But with this freedom came responsibilities.

"Now that all of us have the chance of being primarily medical social workers, we must accept the responsibility which that implies. It is on the quality of our medical social work that we shall be judged. It is on that and that alone that our whole profession must stand or fall". [7]

In the summer of 1948, the Institute of Almoners arranged for more than 40 almoners from all over the country to examine the medical social work task. A very serious and hardworking group, aware of the great opportunity being offered, and of the possible pitfalls, tackled three broad areas of discussion, all related to the almoner as medical social worker:

1. The kind of work the almoner should do now and how it should be selected.

2. The practice of medical social work.

3. The almoner's educational function.

All these issues continued to be discussed, sometimes hotly, certainly with great interest, over the next 26 years.

What the patient and the doctor, as the representative of the multidisciplinary team, had a right to expect from a medical social worker, was summed up by Enid Warren, then Head Almoner at the Hammersmith Hospital: *". . . our first aim is . . . to help the patient to derive the maximum benefit from medical treatment"* (as distinct from the earlier stated aim of *"assisting the doctor in his treatment"*). Patients need in their almoner *"a listener; a well-balanced unbiased person with an informed mind"* – informed on *"people, their behaviour and habits so the medical social worker can show a sympathetic understanding of situations, difficulties and of emotions"*, on *"ailments and diseases"* and on *"community resources"*. The doctor needed someone *"who understands enough about health and ill-health to enable her (the almoner) to appreciate the social implications of each; someone who is cognisant of the structures and resources of the community, knows how society works and how the various resources can be tapped; someone who has been trained in the understanding of people and their reactions to situations of all kinds, and who is prepared to interpret treatment to patients so far as it affects their social life".* [8]

The need for qualified social workers: demand and supply

One of the main problems facing social work in the immediate post-war period was the lack of sufficient numbers of qualified staff and the growing demand for their services from a range of agencies in addition to hospitals. Among the advertisers in the professional journals were:

The Ministry of Labour and National Service, seeking almoners for the Industrial Rehabilitation Centres.
The Miners' Welfare Commission seeking a medico-social worker for the Miners' Rehabilitation Centre at Worksop.
H.M. Colonial Service – for almoners in the Federation of Malaya.
The Medical Research Council for an almoner in a cancer research unit.
The Civil Service Commission – for those with medical social work experience, for posts as Regional Welfare Officers.

At a later date qualified social workers were in demand as members of the Social Work Service of the DHSS (now the Social

Services Inspectorate), Scottish Home Office and DHSS in Northern Ireland and other government departments and as members of the multidisciplinary teams of the Hospital Advisory Service (now the Health Advisory Service).

All these were in addition to many vacancies in hospitals and in Local Authority Health and Welfare Departments, for both almoners and psychiatric social workers.

The issue of recruitment was pursued with vigour and some success by both the Institute of Almoners and the Association of Psychiatric Social Workers during the next 25 years. The five one-year Emergency Courses run by the Institute from 1946 to 1949 in addition to the two-year training programme (described in more detail in Ann Loxley's vignette) added 272 qualified workers to the existing work-force of some 1,000 almoners.

In 1951 two government committees were also tackling these matters. The Cope Committee[9] was charged with the task of examining the need for demand and supply of medical auxiliaries. They included almoners, but not psychiatric social workers. Almoners, together with the occupational therapist and physiotherapist representatives, drew up a minority report which regretted, despite their support for some of the recommendations, that they were unable to support those for registration as members of professions auxiliary to medicine. They noted that the word "auxiliary" in relation to hospital services had come to denote an untrained or partially trained person. They proposed instead the term "Non-medical Professional and Technical Staff". In view of the almoners' emphasis on the importance of education and training, from their inception, this response was hardly surprising. It was a turning point which established almoning as an independent profession.

The Mackintosh Committee, [10] set up to examine similar issues in relation to the mental health services, pointed out that of 333 psychiatric social workers employed in the UK, 65 worked in mental hospitals, 8 in local authority mental health departments, and the remainder divided between out-patient clinics and child guidance services.

Multi-skilled departments

As part of the ongoing debate about the nature of social work, and in response to the continuing shortage of qualified staff, almoners and psychiatric social workers explored the idea of multi-skilled departments. Their starting point was the Ministry of Health

Circular which said *"workers without training and qualifications, who are described as almoners but are doing administrative or clerical work should no longer be referred to as almoners"*. [11]

Since 1948 many hospitals, especially the smaller and provincial ones, had staffed their "Almoners' Departments" with workers holding basic social science diplomas or qualified only by experience. Given the problems of recruitment of qualified staff and the diversity of tasks undertaken by qualified workers as they fulfilled roles of investigator, adviser, broker, advocate, negotiator, counsellor and befriender, the leaders of the profession began to examine the potential for welfare workers in hospitals.

In the mental health services, as the Mackintosh Committee had pointed out in 1951, there were many social workers, some untrained, others with wide variations in both theoretical and practical training, in addition to psychiatric social workers. But with nearly 150,000 people under treatment in hospital, and substantial numbers attending out-patient clinics and child guidance centres, there was a considerable shortage of all workers.

Amongst the urgent measures Mackintosh recommended to increase recruitment were proposals for a trainee scheme. Suitable candidates might apply to become assistants in mental welfare work under the supervision of experienced psychiatric social workers. After a period of two years they would be eligible to apply for entry to a mental health course to qualify as psychiatric social workers. The training included practical experience in local authorities as well as in hospitals.

The almoners took a different approach. In 1957, after discussions within the profession and with the Ministry of Health and Manchester Regional Hospital Board, the Manchester Region introduced a course for Hospital Welfare Workers. Welfare workers would undertake duties in almoners' departments which did not require a casework response. They *"would not be a substitute for almoners, or a superior type of clerk, but another type of social worker, with a distinct function, capable of responsible work"*. In the first two years 12 trainees successfully completed the course.

Mrs Gray, the Tutor-in-Charge of the scheme and herself an almoner, made clear, however, that the scheme would only be fully effective if Head Almoners planned appropriately the use of both almoners and welfare workers in their departments. A number of almoners' departments throughout England began to appoint welfare assistants, though the larger departments, with commitments to teaching almoner students, began to appoint younger workers, often graduates, who after one or two years' experience were expected to go on to professional training. Later, this type of work experience became a requirement for obtaining a place on a social work course. Hospital social work departments became the springboard from which many young workers were launched on their careers.

In 1959 the Working Party on Social Workers in the Local Authority Health and Welfare Services,[12] chaired by Miss (later Dame) Eileen Younghusband reported, recommending a new two-year course of training, which would consist of theory and practice, with supervised fieldwork for about half the time. The Report commented that to some this might seem too short, when teacher training was about to be extended to three years and that for health visitors requiring four years. Specialised training was only desirable if it followed on from general training or was of a higher standard. This was largely an attempt to increase the proportion of qualified workers in the local authority. Many of the students on the first of these courses were very experienced workers seconded by their employers. The overwhelming need was to provide more workers to give a competent social work service for elderly, handicapped and mentally disordered people in areas where there were almost no trained social workers.

The organisation of departments

The Younghusband decision to recommend a new form of training based on *"three categories of users, i.e. complex cases: those who needed a competent social work service: and others who could be serviced by welfare assistants under the supervision of qualified social workers"* added to the continuing debate about referrals and about supervision, which Head Almoners had to consider in managing their departments.

Referrals

Although some hospitals, like St Thomas's in London, produced small booklets about their Social Service Departments perhaps more for the guidance of staff than for patients, there was general concern about access to the almoner for all who might need her help. Was it wise to rely on referred work only, i.e. to rely on others, chiefly doctors and nurses, to recognise the patient's problem and to make contact with the almoner? Would referrers, including patients and their relatives, know how to contact the almoner? Almoners recognised that they had to be proactive: to work in an integrated manner with other professionals in the hospital and in the community, and on occasion work through the caring team without themselves seeing the patient.

By this time there were few who advocated the need to see every patient. Discussion in ward meetings, rather than on ward rounds, was more usual, and through the social workers' contribution to the education and training of medical students and nurses understanding began to grow of the ways in which social workers would use relationships with patients and their families to help them manage the impact of illness and hospitalisation. There were certainly no formal screening or assessment procedures, and no allocation meetings. Social workers were generally linked to specific wards or medical "firms" and dealt with each referral as it came in, exercising some control through regular meetings with the multi-disciplinary team on the wards. Early on, hospital social workers had to learn how to function as independent professionals in the eyes of the rest of the multidisciplinary team. On a day-to-day basis, they were seen as the experts in their field and had to take personal responsibility for assessing a situation, giving professional judgement or suggesting a plan, often in a very short time. The link with firms and the need for prompt action on many referrals, often in a crisis situation, rendered any system of allocation meetings impracticable. At the same time recognition was given to the services provided by the welfare assistants and clerks.

This aspect of hospital social work, with each member of the team making a contribution as needed to the care of the patient, could be highly rewarding, with a real feeling of shared effort on behalf of the patient. It could also sometimes be frustrating when the conflicting demands of pressure on beds for new patients and the well-being of the current patient had somehow to be balanced. Some consultants were very socially minded and greatly valued the extra dimension which social workers brought to the total care of patients; others were less easy to work with and were more likely to see social work input as a possible hindrance to the speedy discharge of patients. Nursing staff varied: some found it difficult to accept an area of patient care with which they were not directly involved; more usually the ward sister and the almoner colluded in the patient's interest. Ward sisters were powerful people, who could be relied upon to protect the patient from premature discharge when plans needed a little more time to come to fruition – "over my dead body" was music to an almoner's ears. By and large the work was deeply satisfying, with a shared consideration of the patient's needs and respect for the other's expertise.

Supervision

A controversial innovation in some forward-looking departments was the practice of staff supervision. This was not simply the overseeing of new staff members, their standards of work and behaviour. It was a process of enabling them to develop their basic skills and to continue their professional learning by means of regular discussions about selected cases with a more experienced and qualified worker.

In 1954 the Institute of Almoners, in collaboration with the Family Welfare Association, arranged for a very experienced social worker from Chicago, Mary Louise Allen, to provide individual supervision for four almoners and eight FWA caseworkers on a weekly or fortnightly basis for a period of about seven months. About this time, too, Miss Zucker, Head Almoner of the West Middlesex Hospital Group, appointed Marjorie Moon as the first almoner whose main task was the professional supervision of staff.

Although such posts were never many, the practice soon grew of planning the allocation work so that senior social workers within the hospital department could spend part of their time giving regular supervision to less experienced staff. There was some opposition to the introduction of staff supervision on the grounds that it implied that staff were not competent to work on their own, but those who experienced it viewed it as a personalised form of post-qualifying study. One correspondent to the Journal noted: *"One intriguing point in all the correspondence about supervision and supervisors is that all who write specifically in favour, have first-hand experience of the method, while those against claim none at all."* [13]

To some, consultation was a more acceptable term, for no one really denied the value of discussion of complex or unusual cases. Eventually a team structure was adopted, with the senior member an experienced and qualified social worker. Teams were in various forms, influenced in part by developments in the local authorities.

Group Almoners

About this time modifications were being introduced in the structure of the National Health Service. Hospitals were grouped together under a Hospital Management Committee, rather than a local management committee. With this development came the opportunity to create Group Almoner posts. This provoked some bitter comment from almoners who were already struggling to spread themselves over several hospitals. They felt those in "large comfortable" departments in teaching hospitals ("ivory towers") should uproot themselves and share in the hurly-burly. Others pointed out that their understaffed situation had enabled them with justification to shed the "routine welfare jobs".

What is perhaps surprising to us today is the lack of published material and other evidence to show the volume of demand for service; the outcome of division of labour in the multi-skill departments or information about the outcome for patients who needed routine welfare help. It is surprising given the meticulous ways in which the pioneers had recorded their activities and in the way some departments had argued cogently for additional posts.

Certainly the uneven distribution of workers, both almoners and psychiatric social workers, was of major concern to the professional bodies. In 1959 the Younghusband Report estimated a need for an additional 150 almoners each year to staff new posts and replace wastage in hospitals, plus a further 500 almoners to meet the needs of the local authority services. Three hundred PSWs were also thought to be needed for mental health hospital services with a further 500 for the local authority services.

The Younghusband Report also pointed out that only 44 married women were employed on a part-time basis in the health and welfare departments of the local authorities. Hospitals departments might employ locums, usually full time for short periods, to cover holidays or casual vacancies and occasionally part-time work was available. The wastage of professionally qualified women on marriage or at the birth of children was of great concern. The Association of Part-time Social Workers was formed in December 1959 to enquire into the availability for part-time work among trained social workers and to press for refresher courses to meet the needs of women who wanted to return to social work after a lapse of several years. A study carried out by Helene Curtis and Phyllis Willmott in 1961 concluded that *"to enable married social workers to return more easily to part time work a good deal of re-organisation and adjustment is called for"*.[14] By making it possible for women to work and train, part time, employers were finding a further option for solving their recruitment problems.

Working in local authority departments

On the inception of the NHS there had been an immediate demand for almoners and for psychiatric social workers. Between 1948 and 1955 the number of qualified almoners employed by counties, county boroughs and city local authorities almost doubled – but only from the low figure of 39 to 75.

Work that had begun in TB and VD clinics in some progressive counties such as Buckinghamshire slowly expanded. County almoners were appointed to work with general practitioners, providing a casework service to selected patients and developing supportive services for families in need, as well as for physically handicapped and elderly people.

The range of work continued to expand, as did the number of local authorities employing almoners. By 1961, Surrey County Council had nine almoners working on the prevention of family break-up, while Nottinghamshire, West Sussex and Hertfordshire looked to them to provide casework services.

In 1964 a local authority group of medical social workers (as almoners became known that year) was formed. The group met regularly in London and in the provinces until it disbanded on the formation of the British Association of Social Workers in 1970. The group provided a forum for discussion of the need for services; the potential for growth of professional social work in the local authority; problems of co-operation with colleagues in other disciplines and services; the training of welfare assistants, and so on. The group also provided support to those taking up newly created posts in unfamiliar structures, on their own without the support of social work colleagues. In 1965 the Institute of Medical Social Workers published "The Medical Social Worker in Community Health and Welfare Services". This pointed out that in addition to helping with the less obvious consequences of illness and disablement, and the loss of independence often felt by patients in the community, social workers with background knowledge and experience of the health service were in great demand. Sometimes they took on responsibility for planning and organising welfare services for the local authority; for planning and running in-service training; schemes for staff supervision, and those for combining existing voluntary and statutory services to make available a more comprehensive service alive to changing needs in the community.

Social work and general practice

When the National Health Service came into being in 1948, general practice had seemed an obvious place to employ a medical social worker. In 1948, the Department of Public Health and Social Medicine at the University of Edinburgh set up a project, the object of which was "to determine amongst other things how the medical practitioner and the almoner, working together as a team, can best supply the medical and social needs of a certain community".

Jane Paterson, who was the almoner appointed to the project, wrote: *"In general practice, however, there is a much greater opportunity for doctor and almoner to study together the needs not only of the individual but of the family as a whole, and to provide as a result a much more efficient service. . . . Much preventive social work could be done by the almoner attached to a Health Centre, which might resolve the necessity of attending the hospital for the treatment of illness, which originated to a great extent in the social background of the patient."* [15] (See also Vignette 3.)

In 1954-5, the opportunities for social work in a general practice in Northern Ireland were explored [16] and in 1955, Manchester University Medical School set up a Health Centre, Darbyshire House, which also employed an almoner. In February 1961, Joan Collins, in Cardiff, began a one year project funded by the Nuffield Provincial Hospitals Trust to provide an almoner service to a practice of four family doctors. She demonstrated the need for this kind of service and from her experience also provided comment on the recommendations of the Younghusband Committee on the training and deployment of social workers in local authority health and welfare departments. [17]

In 1963 the Nuffield Provincial Hospitals Trust funded a further project carried out by Forman and Fairbairn in Barnstaple. The primary object of the three year study was to estimate the value, if any, of a medical social worker in a group practice. One of its main conclusions was that *"the development of medico-social care by the introduction of suitably selected trained personnel into the general practice of the future is likely to be more economical and more effective than equivalent investment in developing social services departments working in relative isolation from general practice".* [18] The medical social worker's training in social assessment and knowledge of social services was seen as of particular value.

In 1972 Goldberg and Neill [19] published the results of the Caversham Project – a four year study of a social work attachment to a group general practice in north-west London which aimed systematically to *"study in action the contribution a social worker can make to the identification and treatment of psycho-social problems in general practice".* Again, it confirmed the need for this kind of work and commented, as the earlier studies had done, on the interplay of physical symptoms and social situations. It also reflected, more than the previous studies, on the relationship between the social worker and the doctors, as well as with other members of the multi-disciplinary team. Inspired by participation in a residential workshop sponsored by the Royal College of General Practitioners, National Institute for Social Work Training and Council for the Education & Training of Health Visitors, in London in March 1972, June Huntington, a sociologist, began a two year study of social work and general practice in Australia. She was "seeking a sociology of inter-occupational relationships" and provided a valuable analysis of all aspects of working together. By the time her study, Social Work and General Medical Practice, was published in 1981, she felt little effective progress had been made, because most practitioners remained unconvinced, not so much of the likely potential for better care, but of the possibilities of making collaboration work in practice.[20] However, in Britain the development of these ideas had to await a later date, as no funding was available. General practitioners, although independent contractors, could not afford to employ social workers. Reorganisation of the National Health Service and of local government was looming and with it the transfer of social workers from the health service to the employment of local authorities.

Co-operation and collaboration – getting on together

Relationships between social workers based in hospitals and their opposite numbers in the health and welfare services in the community, though clearly crucial to good practice, were not always as cordial as they might have been. There were staff shortages and acute pressure of work on both sides and little time to appreciate the other's contribution. The trend towards care in the community continued. Reports from independent and official sources were followed by legislation and new policies that could not be ignored. The advantages of collaboration were quick to emerge. For example, in an area where relations between hospital and community-based workers were good, co-operation between geriatrician and hospital and county almoners *"led to a transformation of the local geriatric service. All patients in the ward and all those on the waiting list were re-assessed. The result was that an impossible waiting list was cancelled and replaced with an effective system of acute admissions. For those who could be discharged home, support for families was assured and a short-term respite care scheme was established"*.[21]

At the Annual General Meeting of the Institute of Medical Social Workers in 1967, the Minister of Health, the Rt. Hon. Kenneth Robinson, warmly acknowledged the importance of the work of the hospital social worker, *"recognising their ability to rapidly identify underlying personal and social factors in the causes of illness and to work towards resolving any family and individual problems which might delay a return to health"*. He also emphasised the need to look forward and to take the long view to meet the growing need in the community. *"There has always been scope for medical social workers outside the hospital service. . . . I am glad to know that [medical social workers] have recognised and are accepting the opportunity to play their part in building up community services."*[22]

In the three years from 1967 to 1970 the number of qualified medical social workers in local authority health or welfare departments rose by nearly two-thirds, from 80 to 130. The need for psychiatric social workers to staff local authority mental health services was also great.

Research

From time to time the professional bodies had engaged one of their number to carry out special studies and practitioners published articles about their work in the journals, but generally speaking there was not a strong tradition of academic research. Interest was engendered in this area in the early sixties, however, when the Institute of Almoners set up a research project to enquire what happened to a group of newly qualified medical social workers in their first two years of practice. This was still a time when for women possibly marriage, and certainly the arrival of children, meant leaving employment. The Institute was interested in making the first two years of practice rewarding enough for almoners to return later. The participants found their interviews with Miss Marjorie Moon very stimulating, as is shown in the report "The First Two Years". [23] Although Harriet Bartlett on a visit to England in 1961 had commented, *"I found casewoork clearly established in British thinking, teaching and practice"* and *"you are working to strengthen casework and develop a generic approach in education"*, [24] for the newly qualified workers in Miss Moon's study, it was working in a setting where social work was not the primary discipline, which at one and the same time made the greatest difficulties and the greatest challenge.

In the fifties and sixties, a few almoners and psychiatric social workers began again to write about the nature of their work. Some small empirical studies were done by individual practitioners. Research studies on the whole had to await the formation of the Research Unit at NISW under Miss E.M. Goldberg, a psychiatric social worker, and interest from the (then) Department of Health and Social Security.

Education and Training for Medical and Psychiatric Social Work: 1946-1970

Education and training were recognised from the outset as necessary prerequisites for employment as an almoner or psychiatric social worker. Considerable attention was given to the content and pattern of training and to recruitment.

During six arduous years Miss A.B. Read had drawn together the Institute of Hospital Almoners' diverse regional training activities and had *"done more than anyone else not only to keep training going, but also to raise the standard"*. In 1946 she moved to become the Head Almoner at St Thomas's Hospital, succeeding Miss Cherry Morris. The Institute of Almoners appointed Miss Helen Rees as Director of Training. Under her auspices the Institute's own training course became one of integrated theory and practice.

Students spent two days each week at lectures and tutorials and three days in hospital placements. It is worth recalling that at that time the Institute was unique in insisting that its students should have a university social science qualification before embarking on professional training. The Tutorial department of three tutors and the Director, carried responsibility for recruitment and selection of students, for planning fieldwork placements, for providing courses for student supervisors, in addition to running two concurrent training courses which produced 60-70 students each year or 343 almoners between 1946 and 1949.[25]

At the same time, as part of the effort to meet the post-war demand for more trained staff, the Institute, backed by the whole profession, decided to run, as an experiment, an emergency course lasting one year. Successful candidates were eligible for the full Almoner's Certificate. Courses were primarily intended for men and women aged between 25 and 35 years, of good intelligence and personality and some relevant experience, which included service in the armed forces and other forms of national service. This "great experiment", as Sir Alan Moncrieff described it, turned out to be five courses, enriching the profession between 1946 and 1949 by 272 certified almoners from 284 candidates. The credit for this successful venture belongs to Miss Kit Stewart (Mrs Russell) and the distinguished Emergency Course Committee under the chairmanship of Miss Cherry Morris. The magnitude of this achievement can be better understood by recalling that the total number of qualified almoners in 1945 was just over 1,000. [26]

The desirability of a common basic training for their two fields and the need to develop a more scientific approach to social work had been discussed by almoners and psychiatric social workers in a meeting in 1944. They were shared in a wider forum in 1946, when the British Federation of Social Workers organised a conference, described as the first common study of training content and method. An idea emerged for an "Institute of Practical Social Studies" to promote standards of fieldwork training and research an idea that lived on in one way or another and probably contributed to the founding of the National Institute of Social Work Training, as it was first known.[27]

In 1948 the British Conference on Social Work recommended that universities should provide professional training as a one year course to follow social science courses – perhaps the first attempt to secure a three year university education for social workers. The Conference also proposed that training should not remain the responsibility of the professional bodies and that caseworkers, groupworkers and personnel workers in industry should share a one year common course. Miss Helen Rees, Director of Training at the Institute of Almoners, was one of those who worked tirelessly for the establishment of generic social work courses in universities.

The Younghusband report on workers in local authority health and welfare services recommended a new, two year non-graduate training course. While many of the students on these courses were social workers without qualifications but with considerable experience, the courses also attracted mature people, often of high calibre, from other fields of employment. Again, hospital departments were much in demand for fieldwork placements, and sometimes profited from their work in terms of recruitment.

Meanwhile the Institute of Almoners had set up a Committee of Inquiry under the chairmanship of the Hon Eleanor Plumer of St Anne's Society, Oxford, to cover the whole field of work.[28] Its report (unpublished) in 1949 contained two far-reaching recommendations: that the Institute should press for adequate financial help for training and a third year of professional training should be included in a full university course in social work. Success on the first issue came in 1953, when the Ministry of Education and the Department of Health in Scotland set aside moneys for grants to students in their final year.

In 1954 the first university course in medical social work started at Edinburgh University, headed by Jean Snelling from the Institute of Almoners. Five years later, when the course was well established, she returned to the Institute to succeed Helen Rees as Director of

Studies, and remained there until 1971, when the Institute's course closed.

The Applied Social Studies course at the London School of Economics also began in 1954. Known as the Carnegie course after its principal funder, it equipped social workers for employment in a range of settings. Its style of training was very much influenced by social work educational practice in the United States of America, using psychodynamic theory and a particular method of supervision which required students to make detailed process recordings of their interviews with patients. This supervisory style soon became standard practice on the Institute course also.

In 1967 the Ministry of Health took on the role of promoter for, after all, social workers were part of a public service, while a growing number of universities became providers of professional courses. The Institute of Medical Social Workers (as the Institute of Almoners was renamed in 1964) however, remained the principal promoter and provider of training for medical social work until its demise.

Education and training for psychiatric social work, which began with the mental health course at LSE in 1929, had expanded, so that by 1968 there were 20 courses of various patterns and length in universities throughout the UK, approved by the Association of Psychiatric Social Workers for the training of psychiatric social workers. Of the 111 students who qualified that year, 60 were graduates, 18 were over 40 years old and seven paid for their training from their own resources. Some 45 suitable students could not be accepted for lack of places on courses, a problem exacerbated by difficulties in finding and funding adequate numbers of supervisors (fieldwork teachers).[29] This was in spite of the growing practice of employing experienced senior social workers, whose main task was to supervise groups of social work students in units, largely in medical or psychiatric settings.

The Trainee Scheme which had given graduates the opportunity to test their suitability for psychiatric social work was terminated in 1968. APSW continued to advise graduates of available opportunities, but their suitability for employment from then on rested with employers. It was anticipated that in the post-Seebohm era of local authority social services departments from 1971 a similar scheme might be initiated to cover the whole range of social service agencies.

In another sense, too, education and training influenced professional practice and attitudes. When the Certificate in Social

Work was introduced in 1962 in response to the recommendations of the Younghusband committee,[30] both medical and psychiatric social workers provided practice placements. Students were accorded the same professional status and expectations as those from longer-established university courses, thus averting battles about a two tier structure or second class workers.

Developments in training elsewhere did not pass unnoticed. Some almoners and psychiatric social workers began to feel they needed to be "more adequately equipped for work which required insight into the emotional problems of our patients". Many almoners found this an unnecessary and alarming statement. "The Almoner" contained letter after letter for and against the new ideas about social work practice and lengthy discussions took place.[31] With two-way traffic across the Atlantic – British almoners and psychiatric social workers widening their horizons and developing their skills in the USA, and senior American social workers, such as Harriet Bartlett, Charlotte Towle and Bess Dana, coming to the UK to share their skills – the "psycho-dynamic camp" gained ground steadily. Psychodynamic thinking offered new explanations of human behaviour; it offered understanding of a patient's inner world. It is perhaps difficult in 1995 to appreciate the impact of such thinking. Much has since been criticised, though many of those ideas are now an accepted part of everyday practice and part of later developments in social work. At the same time, ideas in sociology were being developed and role theory became influential in social work.

The need for a statutory independent council for training was met in 1971 with the formation of the Central Council for Education and Training in Social Work (CCETSW), but although some objectives had been achieved, it was not all good news. The continued ambivalence of the universities to providing professional training was probably underestimated, as was the extent of ambivalence in the wider social services.[32]

The Age of Reorganisation: 1968-1973
Changing times – Kilbrandon, Seebohm and Green Papers

The fifties had been the years when the country slowly emerged from war and established the Welfare State; the sixties grappled with the scope and content of the welfare services; how best to organise, manage and deliver services became the focus of attention.

In 1964, in Scotland, the Kilbrandon Committee[33] proposed the abolition of juvenile courts, to be replaced by lay panels and supported by "a matching field organisation". After review and discussion, and much lobbying of MPs by social workers – their first venture of this kind – the Social Work (Scotland) Act received the Royal Assent in July 1968. The new unified local authority social work departments – which had responsibility for probation officers but not for NHS medical and psychiatric social workers – came into being on 17 November 1968. This Act included at Section 12 a "general duty of welfare", which could be, and was, interpreted very broadly and required that Directors of Social Work should be professionally qualified social workers.

The terms of reference of the Seebohm Committee [34] were "to review the organisation and responsibilities of the local authority personal social services in England and Wales, and to consider what changes are desirable to secure an effective family service".

This did not cover social workers who were employed in the health service, but the Committee noted the high proportion of qualified staff in hospitals, and also commented that a separately organised group of social workers was not helpful in providing continuity of care.

The main recommendation of the Seebohm Committee was that each local authority should have a single unified social service department. Another major recommendation was that the pattern of specialisation in employment should be radically altered. While recognising that the organisation and responsibilities of social work in hospitals were outside its terms of reference, the Committee pronounced itself *"in no doubt . . . [they] should be reviewed urgently in the light of our proposals"*.

In 1962 eight major associations of social workers had begun to look into the benefits of being part of one professional association. The Standing Conference of Organisations of Social Workers (SCOSW) set up the Seebohm Implementation Action Group (SIAG) in October 1969, to demonstrate support for the formation of the new departments and to press for the necessary legislation. SIAG was very active in lobbying government in an endeavour to get all the major recommendations enacted.

The Local Authority Social Services Bill passed through all its stages in 1970 – rushed through before the general election – and the new social services departments came into being in April 1971. One can only speculate what might have happened had the Bill not reached the statute book before that election. As it was, at that time the new departments did not have a responsibility to provide a social work service to hospitals, and medical and psychiatric social workers remained as a separate group for the next three years.

In parallel with SCOSW and SIAG, members of the Institute's Council worked very hard in the last days of its existence on the future of hospital social work departments. Representatives of the Institute were invited to the Department of Health and Social Security to discuss its memorandum of November 1969 to the Secretary of State.[35] The DHSS representatives particularly wished to discuss the arguments which had led the majority of medical social workers to support being employed by the local authorities, while a minority preferred to remain with the authorities to be responsible for the health services. The Department had not made any statement following this meeting as it was expected that their policies would be incorporated in the second Green Paper.

The second Green Paper on the Health Service was published in 1970 and, although a discussion document, it seemed plain that some decisions had already been made. The government had decided *"that services should be organised according to the main skills required – health authorities where the primary skill was that of health care and local authorities where the primary skill was in social care or support".*[36] *"Social workers would be made available by the local authority to serve the hospitals or the Community Health Services centred on the local authority. There would be advantages in efficiency, flexibility, career prospects and continuity if social workers who gave a substantial proportion of their time to work in the health service were seconded to the area health authorities."*

It seemed clear that medical social workers would become a part of the newly established departments of social services when the necessary consultation and legislation had been completed.

Professional associations

In the years between 1946 and 1970 the two main professional associations in the field of social work and health care made an immense contribution to the development of services and to professional practice. Both the Institute of Almoners and the Association of Psychiatric Social Workers, through meetings and journals, provided members with professional support, guidance on practice, help in relation to salaries and conditions of service, setting standards and maintaining the professional registers. They engaged in social action, drawing attention to the needs of users, submitting evidence and working parties and demonstrating new ways of providing services.

The professional bodies had some notable general secretaries. In the early years of the Institute of Almoners, Margaret Roxburgh, with skill and diplomacy, established good relations with the Ministry of Health and the Royal Colleges of Physicians and Surgeons. Marjorie Steel encouraged the regional structure of the Institute of Almoners, through which almoners from all over the country could be involved both in local activities and on national committees. Ann Kelly worked hard for better almoner salaries and grading and played a large part in the Institute's closure and the formation of the British Association of Social Workers.

Working members also made their mark on policy. Almoners in paediatric units in the fifties were concerned about the separation of children in hospital from their parents. Spurred on by the powerful film "A Two Year Old Goes to Hospital" made by James and Joyce Robertson, two psychiatric social workers, they were key movers in the setting up of the National Association for the Welfare of Children in Hospital (NAWCH), whose campaigning led to more-enlightened policies on visiting and many other matters.

Although often mocked as the handmaidens of doctors, the links almoners and psychiatric social workers forged with members of the medical profession and other lay people were invaluable. Far from creating dependency, the capacity to involve others and to value an external view of one's profession was a sign of maturity. By 1970 as they prepared to surrender their specialist identities to the new comprehensive social work association, the British Association of Social Workers, it was with a sense of a great deal achieved, an expectation of good things to come and not a little mourning for the old order, that they moved forward.

The year 1970 was a time of a new apparent confidence in social work. Following the success of Standing Conference of Organisations of Social Workers (SCOSW) and The Seebohm Implementation Action Group (SIAG) hopes for the newly formed British Association of Social Workers (BASW) were high. Oxford House, the premises of the Association of Psychiatric Social Workers, was used by BASW for work relating to its journals and membership, while 42 Bedford Square, the headquarters of the Institute of Medical Social Workers, became BASW's Registered Office on 1 October 1970. The journals of the predecessor associations and "Case Conference" ceased publication and were replaced by new journals "Social Work Today" and the "British Journal of Social Work". The new association had a branch and regional structure through which practising social workers could participate in the professional association's activities and policy-making and providing a local arena for meeting other social workers, planning local initiatives and gaining support.

Kenneth Brill, LLB, AAPSW, General Secretary Designate, had taken up his post on 1 October 1969. Three Assistant General Secretaries were appointed, all of whom were professionally qualified and experienced social workers: Keith Bilton, Secretary of ACCO; Margaret Dobie, Secretary of APSW; and Ann Kelly, Secretary of IMSW. For the next year, these officers were very occupied with the great amount of detailed and complicated planning which had to be done on both domestic and professional issues to establish the new association and to wind up the predecessor bodies. The first meeting of the Council of the British Association of Social Workers took place on 12 June 1970. Enid Warren, last President of the Institute of Medical Social Workers and Vice-Chairman of SCOSW, was voted Chairman.

Medical and psychiatric social work: moving out of the National Health Service

The early seventies were years of change and consultation as social workers developed the new social services and considered and responded to government proposals for the reorganisation of both local government and the NHS. There were many heated debates among social workers and others about the future of hospital social work. Clearly the impetus was for both medical and psychiatric social work to become part of the local authority service.

In March 1972, BASW held a national conference on "The Future of Health Service Social Workers", at which papers were presented giving the range of views, followed by an afternoon of animated discussion. At this time the new social services departments in England had been in existence for only 11 months. The early confusions and unevenness of services were very much in the minds of the meeting. Miss Kelly, acknowledging that there were undeniable risks in integration, also said: *"It is important that people should let the working party set up by BASW have their reasoned views so that it could reasonably prepare the policy statement which Sir Keith Joseph* [Secretary of State for Social Services] *is waiting to receive."*[37]

One of the concerns of the BASW working party on Health Service Reorganisation was that "the distribution of social workers in hospitals is extremely uneven. Of 300 Hospital Management Committees, 74 have no qualified social workers, 93 have no full-time medical or psychiatric social workers. Hospitals in the north of England are less well staffed than those in Greater London and the south". It was thought that if each local authority had responsibility to provide a social work service to the NHS, the service to patients would improve. Later that year BASW Council recommended to the DHSS that area health boards should contract with local authority social service departments to provide a social work service.

On 27 February 1973 the Secretary of State for Scotland announced that social work staff in the health service would be transferred to local authority employment at the time of local government reorganisation in May 1975, a year after the reorganisation of the NHS had taken place. On 28 March 1973 the Secretary of State for Social Services announced the government's decision for England: "social work support for the health service should from 1 April 1974 [the date of local government and NHS reorganisation in England and Wales] be provided by local authority social service departments. Hospital social workers should from that date be employed by local authorities and made available to the health service". The Secretary of State for Wales made the same decision.

In Northern Ireland too consultation and planning for the reorganisation of the health and personal social services were taking place, but in a very different climate. As Rene Boyd pointed out in her history of Social Work in the Royal Victoria Hospital, Belfast: *"At any time change has its difficulties but against the background of the burning, the rioting and the bombings of 1969-1972 social workers in the Royal, as elsewhere, found it hard to concentrate on the new generic identity of their profession and the strategic issues surrounding the massive changes to take place in the organisation of Health and Personal Social Services in Northern Ireland in October 1973."* [38]

Yet they did: in Northern Ireland and in the wider scene. From 1 October 1973 the management of the hospital social services departments was transferred to the district social services office for the geographical area in which the hospital was sited. A principal social worker (health care) based at the district office became responsible for all the social workers based in health settings in the district. Four health and social services boards, covering 17 districts, were accountable to Parliament for the provision of integrated health and personal social services throughout the province.

To take forward the proposals for England and Wales, a "broadly based working party, representing both health service and local authority interests" was set up under the chairmanship of Mr G. J. Otton in August 1973. Its task was to "examine the practical arrangements for the provision of social work support for the health service by the local authorities."[39] This working party looked at the detail of carrying through the recommendations of the earlier working party on collaboration (between NHS and local authority services), which had concluded that *"collaboration between the two services (NHS and Local Authority) would develop most effectively if the professional skills upon which they relied were concentrated in the most appropriate service – medical, nursing and dental skills in the NHS, and social work skills in the Local Authority".*[40]

Because of the need for guidance, especially on matters relating to staff, some decisions were taken and advice was provided in advance of the main report. On 1 November 1973 a consultation paper was published and led to the Staff Transfer Order and in December 1973 the Otton working party recommended the appointment of a "Senior Officer" within each local authority *"to be specially responsible, under the Director of Social Services, for the provision of social work support to the area health authority".*

The Department of Health and Social Security issued a circular[41] giving guidance as to what should be done. An interim report was issued early in March 1974, just weeks before the transfer was due to take place.[42]

The main report was not published until June 1974, three months after the transfer had taken place. The local authority associations had given assurances that they would await the report before taking any action with regard to these responsibilities. The Otton Report made a number of observations and recommendations in order to meet the overriding objective to provide a structure which would integrate social work support to hospitals and general practice with the full range of local authority social services. A second main objective was to promote team-work between social workers, doctors and nurses. The report made clear that, especially in specialist hospital units, there was a need for an on-the-spot service.

Thus, for the first time, a statutory duty was laid upon local authorities to provide social work support to all branches of the NHS, wherever need presented itself. The objective was much more consistent service throughout the NHS than had previously existed, and in theory made it possible for social work help to be available to anyone in any hospital or other health setting. Social workers were to transfer to the employment of local authorities but their clerical staff were to remain with the NHS, which also retained responsibility for equipment and accommodation.

It was expected that the new arrangements would also give hospital-based social workers much greater access to local authority resources and that this too would be of great benefit to service users. However, local authorities had already faced major changes three years earlier, when their existing separate services were integrated, and it was to be expected that yet another change would not be without its teething troubles.

References

[1] Royal College of Physicians: Report on Social and Preventive Medicine, 1943

[2] Medical Social Work, Vol. 18, February 1966, p.282

[3] Davison, E.H., Social Casework, Bailliere, Tindall & Cox, London, 1965

[4] Kelly, A.D., The Almoner, Vol. 14, November 1961, p.349

[5] Bevan, A. The Almoner, Vol. 1, April 1948, pp.5-6

[6] Ministry of Health, Hospital Almoners, 1946 HMC (48)53/BG(48)57

[7] Beck, F., The Almoner, Vol. 1, June 1948 p.53

[8] Warren, E.C., The Almoner, Vol. 4, May 1951, p.73

[9] Cope Report, Report of the Committees on Medical Auxiliaries, Cmnd 8188, 1951

[10] Mackintosh Report, Report of the Committee on Social Workers in the Mental Health Services, Cmnd 8260, 1951

[11] Ministry of Health, ibid

[12] Younghusband, E.L., Report of the Working Party on Social Workers in the Local Authority Health and Welfare Services, Ministry of Health, 1959

[13] The Almoner, Vol. 7, March 1955, p.471

[14] Part-time employment, some aspects of recruitment and training in social work: an enquiry in London. Helene Curtis and Phyllis Willmott, 1961

[15] The Almoner, Vol. 1, February 1949, pp.232-3

[16] The Almoner, Vol. 7, December 1954

[17] Medical Social Work, Vol. 20, April 1967, p.23

[18] Forman, J.A.S. and Fairbairn, E.M., Social Casework in General Practice, Nuffield Provincial Hospitals Trust, Oxford University Press, 1968

[19] Goldberg, E.M. and Neill, J., Social Work in General Practice, George Allen and Unwin, 1972

[20] Huntington, J., Social Work and General Medical Practice – Collaboration or Conflict? George Allen and Unwin, 1981

[21] Raven, H. Personal Communication

[22] Medical Social Work, Vol. 18, July 1965, p.119

[23] Moon, E.M. and Slack, K. The First Two Years, The Institute of Medical Social Workers, 1965

[24] Bartlett, H., The Almoner, Vol.15, July 1962, p.97

[25] Snelling, J.M., The Contribution of the Institute of Medical Social Workers to Education for Social Work, Association of Social Work Teachers, 1970

[26] Institute of Almoners, Report on Emergency Courses of Training for Almoners 1946-1949, September 1949

[27] Snelling, J.M., ibid

(28) Plumer, E., Report of a Committee of Inquiry (unpublished) reported on in The Almoner, Vol. 6, November 1953, p.379

(29) Association of Psychiatric Social Workers, Annual Report, 1968

(30) Younghusband, E.L., The Report of the Working Party on Social Workers in the Local Authority Health and Welfare Services, HMSO, 1959

(31) The Almoner, 1955, onwards

(32) Snelling, J.M. ibid

(33) Kilbrandon, Report of the Committee on Children and Young Persons (Scotland) Cmnd 2306 Edinburgh, HMSO, 1964

(34) Seebohm, Report of the Committee on Local Authority and Allied Personal Social Services, Cmnd 3703 London, HMSO, 1968

(35) The Institute of Medical Social Workers, The Future of Hospital Social Work Departments – A Memorandum to the Secretary of State, IMSW November 1969

(36) Second Green Paper on the proposed restructuring of National Health Service, England only, para 31 and para 46, HMSO, February 1970

(37) Social Work Today, Vol. 3, 6 April 1972, p.8

(38) Boyd, I.F., Social Work in the Royal Victoria Hospital, Belfast, 1938-1988 undated but available in 1988

(39) Otton Report, Social Work Support for the Health Service – Report of the Working Party, HMSO, London, 1974

(40) Report of the DHSS Sub-committee Working Party on Collaboration between Area Health Authorities and Local Authorities

(41) LASSL (73) 47: Welsh Office Circular 5/74

(42) LASSL (74) 5: Welsh Office Circular 73/74

EDUCATION AND TRAINING

Helen Rees,
Director of Studies,
Institute of Almoners
1946-1958

London Hospital Almoners 1958
Grade Dedman (back left)

Jean Snelling, Director of Studies, Institute of Almoners, 1958-1971 (centre)
with students on the Medical Social Work Course, Edinburgh

*Ann D. Kelly, OBE,
last General Secretary of
IMSW and one of the
first Assistant General
Secretaries of BASW*

*Enid C. Warren, OBE,
last President of IMSW
and first
Chairman of BASW
1970-71*

FROM INSTITUTE OF MEDICAL SOCIAL WORKERS, ASSOCIATION OF PSYCHIATRIC SOCIAL WORKERS TO BRITISH ASSOCIATION OF SOCIAL WORKERS

Kay McDougall, OBE, Chairman of SCOSW, watched by David Jones, Margaret Dobie, Enid Warren and George Pratt, signs the Articles of Association of BASW, 24 April 1970

Left: Kenneth Brill, CBE, LIB, AAPSW, PhD, first General Secretary of BASW 1970-74

Right: Mary Windsor, AMIA, Principal Officer (Health) Westminster SSD, twice President of the International Federation of Social Workers

THE CENTENARY YEAR

Baroness Faithfull launches the Year and unveils a plaque to Mary Stewart at the Royal Free Hospital, 18 January 1995

Among those attending the launch were Luana Howard, Sheila Hart, Doris Thornton, Marjorie McInnes, Eileen Turner-Smith (last Chairman of IMSW), Phyllis Willmott, and in front Hazel Osborn and Joan Baraclough

Left to right: at the ceremony in the hospital's Sheila Sherlock Suite are the four principal social workers who have been employed at the hospital since 1939: Sheila Hart (1939-1971), Ann Francis (1971-1987), Rosemary Dinnage (1987-1992) and Diane Brown (since 1992)

Stand prepared by hospital social workers in South-East Staffordshire SSD displayed in Burton General Hospital, September 1995

PARLIAMENTARY RECEPTION

The Secretary of State for Health, the Rt Hon Virginia Bottomley MP

David Hinchliffe MP, host of the Parliamentary Reception, welcoming the guests

The Secretary of State for Health with Baroness Faithfull

Margaret Beckett MP, Shadow Secretary of State for Health, with Kay Richards, former Chair of BASW

12

PRINCIPLES

of

SOCIAL WORK PRACTICE

These principles have been abstracted from
"A Code of Ethics for Social Work" published by
the British Association of Social Workers
and upheld by all BASW members

- Knowledge, skills, and experience used positively for the benefit of all sections of the community and individuals.

- Respect for clients as individuals and safeguarding their dignity and rights.

- No prejudice in self, nor tolerance of prejudice in others, on grounds of origin, race, status, sex, sexual orientation, age, disability, beliefs, or contribution to society.

- Empowerment of clients and their participation in decisions and defining services.

- Sustained concern for clients even when unable to help them or where self-protection is necessary.

- Professional responsibility takes precedence over personal interest.

- Responsibility for standards of service and for continuing education and training.

- Collaboration with others in the interests of clients.

- Clarity in public as to whether acting in a personal or organisational capacity.

- Promotion of appropriate ethnic and cultural diversity of services.

- Confidentiality of information and divulgence only by consent or exceptionally in evidence of serious danger.

- Pursuit of conditions of employment which enable these obligations to be respected.

User and social worker preparing plans for discharge, 1995

CHAPTER THREE

ONE DOOR – MANY MANSIONS: 1974-1995

Hazel Osborn

The 20 years which make up this period were ones of major economic and social changes in the United Kingdom, which affected and were reflected in social work practice. Few professions have undergone such changes and faced such increasing demands as social work did in this period.

The creation of local authority Social Services Departments (SSDs), with a hierarchical structure of organisation, gave social work a central place in the public services, leading to much greater public expectations. Such expectations, perhaps inevitably, led to a level of media attention not previously experienced in the world of social work. The effect of the media upon the way in which the practice of social work was perceived by the general public was one of the new experiences for social workers in this period of time.

For medical and psychiatric social workers the period began with the greatest change of all, that of moving from a closely knit professional group focusing upon helping sick people into a large social work grouping and from the National Health Service (NHS) to local authority SSDs. From 1974 onwards the responsibilities of SSDs included a service to patients of the NHS and health-related social work began to be the description given to what had formerly been medical and psychiatric social work.

So much change took place in these 20 years that they are more easily considered in the three periods which relate to the major social changes which affected social work:

1974-1980: when the new organisations brought high hopes for social workers but many new organisational demands, not least the introduction of genericism and the apparent abandonment of specialisation.

1980-1990: a period which saw the gradual dismantling of the Welfare State and the development of the mixed economy of welfare with SSDs becoming facilitators rather than direct providers.

1990-1995: a time of much greater user involvement and of care in the community, a time when pressure to define social work and its relationship to society became much more intense.

1974-1980: New Organisations and High Hopes

In 1974 against a background of the first intimations of financial restrictions, and the report of the enquiry into the death of Maria Colwell, health-related social workers became a part of the, still quite new, SSDs (in England and Wales). In 1974 England and Wales local government boundary reorganisation frequently created completely new departments, just as they were settling down after the formation of SSDs in 1971. In Scotland and Northern Ireland, as described in the previous chapter, the timing of the inception of the new departments was rather different.

Social workers began the seventies with a great deal of optimism. They had achieved a largely united social work profession and the new departments of social services had been established. Reasonable resources were available to meet the challenges to the new departments and the number of qualified social workers was increasing.

1966	7,600 fieldworkers	Seebohm Report[1] (Appendix 1)
1973	13,500 fieldworkers	CIPFA Annual Return and DHSS statistics[2]
1974	17,000 fieldworkers	CIPFA Annual Return and DHSS statistics[2]: includes health social workers

Medical and psychiatric social workers entered a much larger field of professional practice and exchanged a national employer for a local authority employer with accountability to local councillors.

With SSDs again facing major organisational problems and new responsibilities through the reform of local government and the reorganisation of the NHS, little time was available in many authorities for consideration of the best ways to organise health-based social work and to relate it to an area-centred service. Most remained based in hospitals. However, there were some exceptions. In Coventry in 1973 all health-based social workers moved into area centres with consequent major disruption to the integrated multi-disciplinary service to clients in the NHS.

In many other areas the organisational changes had little immediate effect on the day-to-day work with patients. At the same time different administrative procedures had to be accommodated: for example, new letter headings giving the name of the social services department as well as the hospital had to be used; letters were written in the third person and signed for the Director of Social

Services instead of in the social worker's own name. Secretarial staff remained employees of the NHS. However, social service departments were soon faced with a shortage of staff to cover increasing workloads, and pressures arose in many places to reduce the time allocated to work in hospitals and other health settings in favour of what were seen as the mainstream services of the departments.

At this time too a climate of anti-élitism was evident both in society and in social work. Health-related social workers with their emphasis upon professional standards, training, a fully qualified service, and a closely knit professional body, together with their close association with the medical profession, were sometimes seen by their colleagues as élitist. They themselves believed that social workers needed sound training and standards in order to offer clients the most effective service, particularly in a setting where well-qualified professionals abounded.

Community social workers from the former welfare departments also had extensive experience of working with disabled and chronically sick people, but very little in working with people who were acutely sick or in life-threatening situations.

The Chronically Sick and Disabled Persons Act 1970[3] had laid the foundations for the provision of services for disabled people. Where local authorities had appointed community occupational therapists (OTs), they largely developed this service. Health-related social workers were not seen as a resource to work alongside the occupational therapists. OTs were regarded as the experts for all work with disabled people, although they themselves had often trained in settings where they and health social workers were part of the same multidisciplinary team.

One of the immediate issues in 1974, that of the way in which health-related social work was to be organised, was taken up at government level in the setting up of the Otton Committee. [4]

In England and Wales local authorities assumed a statutory responsibility for social work support to the NHS as a part of the reorganisation of both the local authorities and the NHS on 1 April 1974. In Scotland it took place on 1 May 1975, a gap of a year between the reorganisation of the NHS and the reorganisation of the local authority, thus medical and psychiatric social workers spent a year in the reorganised NHS before joining the new departments of local authority social work.

In the early post-reorganisation years many authorities appointed a Principal Officer (Health), or similar post, at senior management level as recommended in the Otton Report. The post holder had particular responsibilities for the social work service to the health service but this was interpreted in different ways and often had other responsibilities added to it.

The SSD became responsible for providing social work support to all parts of the NHS where need presented itself. The aim was to have a much more consistent service throughout the NHS than had previously existed. It became possible for social work help to be available to anyone who was a patient of the NHS.

The local authority welfare departments had provided services for people with chronic ill health, but the fact that so many of the problems presented to the SSDs had a health component was not initially realised. Nor did social workers in the wider SSDs realise that there were now social workers in their departments with knowledge and skills in working with the effect and meaning of the experience of acute illness; the onset of disability; death and dying, and working in multidisciplinary settings. It took time for the knowledge and skills possessed by these new members of SSDs to be appreciated and drawn on. It also took time for it to be appreciated that a very high proportion of all social service clients (some say 90%) have problems associated with ill health and that health-related issues might arise in any area of social work.

The hope for the future was to achieve a state where all social workers would have sufficient expertise to recognise and assess the needs of clients whose social and health problems were interrelated; the skills to intervene constructively in situations where ill health was a significant factor and the ability to provide a specialised service where particular expertise was necessary, such as with patients and their families facing life-threatening situations or treatments which created ethical and emotional dilemmas.

The Social Context (1974-1980)

The first financial constraints were felt in SSDs in 1975 and continued for many years. Until the change of government in 1979 there seemed to be a general consensus about the basic tenets of the Welfare State, but government imposed financial constraints began to move policies towards a more-market-based approach in the next decade. This introduced a mixed economy of welfare in which the voluntary and private sectors had a much greater role.

Social changes were beginning to gather momentum. The increase in the number of frail, elderly people living into very old age, increasing unemployment and poverty were becoming apparent, and continued to increase in the following decade.

In health care, there were enormous advances in medical science and much new technology was introduced. Kidney and heart transplants became common: oncology procedures multiplied and infertility treatments developed.

There were changes too in individual relationships with social organisations. The belief that every individual has rights which have to be respected became more widely accepted. This trend was visible in the Race Relations Acts of 1965, 1968 and 1976, and in the Sex Discrimination Act of 1975. Such legislation demonstrated values which social workers had always maintained. Bill Jordan in his paper "Clients are Fellow Citizens"[5], given at the Annual General Meeting of BASW in Edinburgh in 1975 underlined the importance of such values in social work.

Changes in attitudes to care

For people suffering from mental illness, community care initiatives had begun in the fifties largely as a response to new drug regimes. Plans to move people out of large psychiatric hospitals and large hospitals for people with learning difficulties gained greater impetus in the seventies. Planning for care in the community set out in such government documents as Better Services for the Mentally Handicapped [6] and Better Services for the Mentally Ill,[7] was seen as more beneficial for individual patients.

The growing need to plan well for supporting elderly people into great old age was highlighted in the report A Happier Old Age [8] while in 1974, CCETSW's report Social Work: People With Handicaps Need Better Trained Workers,[9] reflected the need to develop training which respected the rights of people with disabilities to be supported to live in the community wherever possible.

In the 1970s community care was largely seen as care *in* the community, with a high level of professional input. By the 1980s it had become, rather, care *by* the community to be delivered by informal carers, usually women, and voluntary and private sector providers.

Social Work in Great Britain (1974-1980)

The organisation of social workers

The delivery of social services through local area social services offices had been in existence for three years before medical and psychiatric social workers joined SSDs, while debates about the nature of genericism and the merits of specialisation began much earlier. These features of the organisation of social services presented some difficulties for health-related social work and the way it was perceived. Since health-related social workers worked with people of all ages and a wide variety of social needs, they could be regarded, and regarded themselves, as generic workers. In that they worked in specialist settings, such as hospitals and child guidance clinics, this perception appeared to run counter to general ideas of genericism.

Social workers in the health service did not appear to be bound by specific, client-focused legislation and their hospital practice was not visible to the mainstream of the SSDs, so that such social work was seen by some as a soft option. The work of hospital social workers was thought by area-based staff to be less demanding than that of the rest of the SSD. This was often more a product of the struggle they had to integrate their practice into the new hierarchical organisation which other social workers had confronted much earlier. In fact with their generic approach and subsequent employment as social workers by the local authority, health-related social workers had the opportunity and authority to undertake the statutory component of social work so making it possible to achieve the objective articulated in the Seebohm Report (para 516) – *"we consider that a family or individual in need of social care should, as far as possible, be served by a single worker".*[10] Health social workers had to become knowledgeable about working with and being accountable for the use of powers under new legislation, as well as about managing this responsibility within the multidisciplinary health team and local authority systems and procedures.

The SSDs' new management structures needed professionally qualified staff to manage at senior levels and many highly qualified and experienced social work practitioners moved into these posts. In all areas of social work this often meant that the least-trained and experienced social workers were exposed to a greatly increased "bombardment" of referrals. At the same time almost all social workers were struggling with the new organisational structures, where success depended upon the individual social worker's capacity to incorporate ideas of genericism and apply his or her own specialist knowledge and skill to a wide variety of client situations. Medical and psychiatric social workers therefore joined departments which were under pressure from a whole range of new situations and where there was little time to consider in what ways their practice might be integrated into the overall service.

Despite the increased number of social workers, there was still a pressing shortage of qualified staff in local authority SSDs. This was particularly marked in some large authorities and in London where social service departments found themselves with the duty to service groups of hospitals, including large teaching hospitals, with well-established and well-staffed departments. In some such cases conflict arose over redeployment of staff and over the financing of work where hospital patients came from a geographical area beyond that of the local authority which employed the social workers. Generally these situations were handled with understanding, but later in the decade when expenditure restrictions began to bite on staffing levels, such pressure increased.

Health social workers entered departments where generally they constituted a relatively small group of the total employed. The new comprehensive social service organisations presented a situation where staff with a range of tasks far wider than the practice of social work had to find ways of working together in pursuit of the well-being of the client.

In the seventies also some social workers moved away from a focus on working with individuals and their families to an emphasis on the social and political context in which they lived. It was suggested that helping based upon a psychodynamic approach could result in clients feeling the source of the problem lay within themselves, when the real source was in their environment or the system in which they lived.

At the time interest in influencing systems appeared new and yet the following quotation demonstrates a long-standing awareness of the pressures of the outer world. Indeed, working with the outer world of clients goes back to the beginnings of health social work.

Robinson, writing in 1982, recalls Harriett Bartlett's comments in 1970: *"In recent years there has been a growing recognition of . . . the need for social work to broaden its efforts in the direction of social policy [and] social planning."* She (Harriett Bartlett) raises the question of whether this implies a distinction between two separate groups in social work, whom she calls respectively "people helpers" and "system changers". Ultimately she rejects this distinction, because her *"examination of practice does not suggest such a two track division between social work operations. It suggests instead that social work has as interventive repertoire comprising a considerable number of measures and techniques which are used in various combinations by practitioners"*.[11] [12]

However, it did seem much more possible to influence national and local systems with a unified professional body from a base in large departments. A dilemma for individual social workers was how far a social worker should support a client in taking some sort of direct action, when that action might be against his or her employing authority. The role of councillors in representing the interests of the authority's residents and as having final responsibility for all local authority employees could occasionally give rise to some complex situations. Such issues might be seen as the forerunners of later situations involving "whistle blowers".

By 1978-9, for the first time social workers were involved in strikes over pay and grading. This was partly fuelled by feelings of disillusion at the withering of the high hopes of better services for clients which existed at the beginning of the decade and a growing awareness of the gap between perceived needs and resources.

Many social workers began to observe that the only way to achieve any career progression was through promotion via the managerial path. This, combined with the view that a review of social work pay was overdue, led equally to a desire for increased pay and for a career grade which would encourage experienced social workers to remain working directly with clients. Social workers thought that clients were suffering because they were often seen by the least experienced social workers and that more highly skilled workers should be available to them. Commitment to working directly with clients, and to developing skills and understanding in that work, should be acknowledged and rewarded. BASW had already pressed very hard for a career grade, up to consultant level, but had not been successful. Levels of pay were dependent upon the resources available rather than upon individual merit.

For social workers to strike was highly unusual. Medical and psychiatric social workers had previously worked with a "no strike" clause in their NALGO membership. Many social workers felt personally driven by the situation. To strike was to some extent part of the prevailing ethos following the Winter of Discontent, but also organisational structures had separated social workers from their professional leaders. Directors of social services had become the people with whom social workers negotiated. For all social workers there was a major ethical issue: "us or our clients". For health-related social workers this was a particularly acute issue. They had always worked in situations where the saving of life meant that without question the patient/client came first. The strikes brought into sharper focus the question of their professional identity. Were they professional social workers first or local government officers? It was for many both a very uncomfortable experience and a defining moment. This situation led many social workers to join a union rather than the professional association. It meant individual decisions about whether to belong to both kinds of organisation and consideration of what each might offer.

All social workers need to establish a professional identity. For medical social workers, who until this time had been employees of the NHS, the position had been clear. Almoners were social workers in a medical setting. The Cope Report of 1951 had helped to establish that almoners were a profession in their own right. The Institute of Medical Social Workers (as the Institute of Almoners became in 1964) maintained a register of medical social workers and approved courses of education and training in universities as conferring eligibility for entry to the register. Staff support and professional development were provided by senior members of the profession (see Chapter 2) and upheld by the professional body which set standards for practice and training.

The demise of the Institute and of the Association of Psychiatric Social Workers which also maintained a register and operated in a similar way, and the need for a strong new association uniting all social workers in the new local authority departments and in other agencies was keenly felt by medical and psychiatric social workers at that time. The diversity and size of the new groupings in the SSDs made establishing an identity in them a major challenge. Social workers in health wanted to be in the wider world but were uncertain, as time went on, whether the needs of users of the health service could be heard in them. The structures were new, or almost new, to everyone. Health-based social workers found themselves in situations where everyone was struggling with his or her inherited stereotypes whilst attempting to respond to the bombardment of new referrals, organisational networks and procedures.

There was for some a particular feeling of betrayal in 1975 when the undertaking made in 1970 that BASW would be an association for qualified social workers was reversed. At the time many others saw this as misplaced élitism. From the beginning, health social work had been developed from the principle that social workers must be trained and qualified if they were to provide the best service to clients and also to maintain an independent and credible place with other agencies.

Health-based practice in the seventies

Medical and psychiatric social workers were experienced in working in multidisciplinary teams and understood the structure and functioning of the health systems. The new SSDs, however, had little understanding or knowledge of the multidisciplinary teamwork within hospitals or other institutional settings and the importance of the contribution health-based social workers could make to patient care and to the education and training of health professionals in dealing with the effects of illness, disability and loss.

The Otton Report had emphasised that *"arrangements designed merely to establish that a social worker can be called when necessary by impersonal communication from one system to the other are not good enough"*.[13] Where this happened the health-based social worker came to be viewed mainly as a channel for the provision of community services and a dealer in social emergencies.

Health-based social workers were used to working in a service which operated 24 hours a day. There were sometimes difficulties in reconciling this with a largely daytime, local government service. Ironically, many health-based social workers found that their new colleagues were under the illusion that hospital social work was very much on a 9 to 5 basis.

Many medical and psychiatric social workers, experienced and skilled in working with and for clients in a multidisciplinary setting found the multidisciplinary aspect of their work rewarding and had extensive experience in their particular fields. They had developed skills in working in groups and networks, and those in hospitals had learnt to work at the interface between hospital and community. This interface demanded skills in negotiation to obtain resources for clients within the NHS and in the community across the catchment area of the hospital or unit. In the new situation where the health-based social worker was a part of the SSD but working in the "host" agency of the NHS, ways of getting resources for clients had to be renegotiated. Area-based social workers following clients into the health base had to be accommodated and access for all social workers to medical notes had to be reconsidered.

The more senior members of the hospital social workers' group had experience of managing, supporting and supervising staff, both in large departments and in scattered bases, as a part of their responsibilities for groups of hospitals. Medical social work had developed a system of support and management to help social workers to continue to develop their social work skills and to do this in settings where pressures might restrict or erode such skills. Experienced and well-qualified managers, who understood and could work with the health system while upholding social work values, were very necessary to the maintenance and development of both health and local authority services at this time, though this was not always recognised by SSDs and on occasion led to stress for social workers and diminution of service.

In 1974 medical and psychiatric social workers were familiar with professional journals which (especially in the late sixties and therefore of recent memory) carried articles written by social workers about practice in very specific fields, such as work with people suffering from mental illness, in child guidance, or with people who had suffered amputation of a limb, or were undergoing renal dialysis or kidney transplant. The correspondence columns of the journals also supported very lively debates about other aspects of practice. Although these papers and discussions were a regular part of medical and psychiatric social workers' experience, they were not as easily available to social workers entering health related social work after 1974 and to a great extent the content of this experience became inaccessible to those who entered the field later. Being part of the wider world of social work for a time led to differing priorities and health-related social work topics had to compete for a place in the new journals.

By 1980, maybe as a response to the generic approach, some of the stereotypes had been modified and many social workers without specialist training had entered the health field. This produced a more emphatic social work approach to multidisciplinary working, but often made it difficult for users, whose interests could be lost whilst social work staff new to the health context attempted to grapple with the intricacies of health systems and whilst they gathered experience in working with the human response to acute illness.

Gains for patients

Although becoming part of the social service departments in 1974 had bewildering aspects for individual social workers, they believed there were gains for patients of the health service

All local authorities now had a responsibility to provide social work support to patients of the NHS. In a number of authorities this meant there were more social workers available to the health base, and it opened up for many patients the possibility of earlier intervention at the most effective crisis point. Some large hospital departments were not able to fill posts due to the financial constraints and long gaps made it difficult to offer a satisfactory service to all units.

There were also gains from continuity with clients and families having to see only one social worker, who could follow them into hospital from the community or from hospital into the community.

Sensitive work with acutely sick people continued and opened up the possibility of greater diversity of service immediately available to patients, and service which could be closely linked to the community in which the patient lived. Group work continued to develop in health bases and the work begun with the families of battered babies in the sixties was further extended in the field of child abuse. The specialised social work in the care of dying people and their families, which had been written about in the Institute Journal 20 years earlier [14] [15] continued to develop both in acute health care and in the new MacMillan continuing care units.

For health-related social workers, the reorganisation in 1974 meant access to resources provided by the local authority to provide a continuity of care for clients. Some social workers in health bases found that they immediately had much easier access to resources; for others it was to take longer to establish access to systems.

Education and training

In 1971 all social work training became the responsibility of CCETSW and all courses were based in educational institutions. The Institute of Medical Social Workers had closed its training school and had negotiated the expansion of places on university courses to maintain the output of qualified social workers. The Certificate of Qualification in Social Work (CQSW) became the only recognised qualification for professional social work for people who qualified from 1971 onwards. CCETSW approved courses and was responsible for the maintenance of standards of training. Some university courses, for example the psychiatric social work course at Manchester University, continued to offer specialist training for some years. Other courses such as that at Southampton University continued to offer specialist options on their courses.

At the same time many local authorities developed their own training sections which provided in-service training. On the whole they had to offer training to meet immediate requirements, often in response to new legislation. They rarely offered training specific to the needs of social workers in the health field. Some training sections seconded staff to qualifying courses.

However, in the mid-seventies CCETSW, in association with local authorities, began the development of a "framework for training, designed to meet the needs of a wide variety of workers in the social services". The Certificate in Social Service (CSS) was introduced.[16]

This was a serious effort to increase the level of training among the staff of the SSDs and voluntary social services. It was envisaged as a possible qualification for a wide range of staff other than social workers and for organisers of domiciliary care. Five pilot schemes were set up in 1975. In 1980 CCETSW published the Regulations and Guidelines for courses leading to the CSS. Schemes were established and continued to develop until 1989. That year both the CSS and the CQSW were replaced by the Diploma in Social Work.

Social work theory

The predominant theories in the seventies, in addition to systems theory, were those of crisis intervention and task-centred work. Crisis intervention always had a particular relevance to the health field ("... *it also struck me that people talk more easily in hospital than elsewhere" (because they are in crisis) – social work student*) because very frequently the social worker entered the situation at the point of a major crisis such as a car accident, following a stroke or where someone was mortally ill.

Task-centred theory, with its emphasis upon agreement with the client/user about the problem to be addressed and negotiating responsibilities for its resolution, might be seen as pointing the way to present-day user empowerment and responsibility. Some of the problems addressed were often the difficulties encountered by clients in claiming welfare benefits. Social workers had to regain expertise in the field of welfare rights whilst not losing sight of the psychotherapeutic aspects of their work.

The coming of the large social service departments made it possible, and imperative, to find ways of making sense of large systems and finding ways of influencing them. Systems theory presented a methodical approach to this new situation, although for health-related social workers finding ways of affecting systems had long been part of their practice.

The professional organisations – BASW, ADSS and IFSW

When the British Association of Social Workers was set up in 1970 the leading members of the constituent associations became key members. Distinguished members of the medical and psychiatric social work professions took leading roles in the new association and for the next three years continued to carry forward the policies which had been agreed before their professional bodies were wound up, in particular those which led to medical and psychiatric social workers becoming a part of SSDs in 1974.

In the first years of BASW some of the professional leaders were appointed Directors of Social Services/Social Work and became members of the newly established chief officers groups, the Associations of Directors of Social Services/Social Work. At first many retained their membership of both associations but this became less usual as time went on. (It was customary in local government to have a chief officers' association which is separate from their professional body.) The effect this had upon a professional association in depriving it of experience and leadership could bear more-detailed discussion in another place.

In the international field of social work, BASW maintained and developed the existing links with the International Federation of Social Workers. Mary Windsor, a qualified medical social worker, head of St Mary's Hospital, London, Social Service Department and later Principal Officer (Health), Westminster SSD, became the first, and so far the only, British president of the IFSW. She was also the only president to date to serve two consecutive terms of office. In her time in office she visited all the major continents, often seeing social workers who were at the time *personae non grata* in the prevailing regime.

BASW's journal, Social Work To-Day (later joined with Community Care) carried articles of current interest and was a forum for professional debate and support. In January 1994 BASW began publishing a new magazine, *Professional Social Work*. From April 1971 BASW also published, and continues to publish, a bi-monthly journal, The British Journal of Social Work, which provides an arena for academic debate and research.

The BASW Special Interest Groups have been a vital part of BASW, providing a professional, rather than an employment, focus for specialist interests and promoting the growth of professional networks.

1980-1990: a Mixed Economy of Welfare

By 1980, when Social Service Departments had been in existence for nearly 10 years, the emphasis upon the *organisation* of social work and social services began to be displaced by public interest in the *practice* of social work. This arose to a great extent from the conflicting and biased impressions of social work offered by the media when reporting high profile situations, usually in the field of child protection.

This interest became more focused when in 1980, at the request of the Secretary of State for Social Services, a working party was set up by the National Institute for Social Work under the chairmanship of Mr Peter M. Barclay to promote, at government expense, *"an independent and authoritative enquiry into the roles and tasks of social workers"*.[17]

The Barclay Committee reported in 1982. The detailed findings stressed the point that social workers were needed to *"plan, establish, maintain and evaluate social care and to provide counselling"*. The twin skills of social care planning and counselling were emphasised. The report also commented upon social work partnerships with users, informal carers and voluntary bodies. In recommending a *"community approach"* the committee described community social work as implying *"a focus on individuals and families set in the context of all the networks of which they do, or might, form part"*.

The trends for the eighties were becoming clearer.

The context of social work

Throughout the eighties major changes took place in the social and political frameworks in which social work was practised. A market economy became established and the pressure on resources made the gap between needs identified and needs met much more pronounced. It became increasingly important to focus resources where user's needs were seen as greatest.

In parallel with these changes the concept of the individual's rights and responsibilities continued to develop. The Data Protection Act 1984 embraced the same principles as had been contained in the Institute of Almoner's document on confidentiality in 1947, that records should be accurate, relevant, and only kept as long as needed. The Act also recognised the client's right to see his/her file. For health-related social workers the fact that there had to be separate arrangements for access to medical notes and social work records did not help co-operation and a holistic approach to the care of sick people. The difficulties and anxieties which attended these changes meant that in some places social workers working in the health field finally ceased to contribute to medical records or to consider that they had relevance to their work, whereas others made greater use of records to convey the patients' needs and often wrote them in conjunction with the patient.

The Patients and Citizens Charters also established users' rights but expected individuals to take personal and financial responsibility for themselves. In the latter half of the eighties the Patients Charter for achieving quality assurance in the NHS prompted agencies and the NHSME and the Social Services Inspectorate to develop usable methods of evaluating the outputs of the service and to give more valuable information about the outcomes of NHS care.

The decade ended with the publication of various White Papers, Consultative Documents and government guidance: "Working for Patients, The Health Service, Caring for the 1990s" (1989) and "Community Care: Agenda for Action" (1988) (the Griffiths report). These re-emphasised the need for local authorities to take on a more enabling role and to work in partnership with users, carers, voluntary bodies and the private sector.

At the same time, arising out of developments in the field of child protection and their responsibilities under the Children Act 1989 an emphasis was laid on partnership with parents. This legislation brought changes in the organisation of social work in area teams, with social workers much more clearly deployed in teams working with either adults or with children.

One of the major issues in this decade was the care of very elderly, frail people. The number of long term beds within the NHS was being reduced and there was a dramatic increase in the number of privately run nursing and residential homes, directly encouraged by the government policy of subsidising those on very basic incomes (that is State pension plus supplementary benefit) with weekly maintenance payments. At the same time, those who owned their homes were often encouraged by medical and nursing staff to sell them, sometimes causing hardship to remaining members of their families. In the health service, Elderly Care Units specialising in the treatment of acutely ill elderly people became more numerous, whilst long stay wards were phased out. Advances in medical care in these years and major organisational changes inevitably brought many dilemmas and challenges to social workers in the health field.

The organisation of health care changed dramatically between 1980 and 1990. In the acute sector the length of time people remained in hospital was significantly reduced.

"National statistics confirm the accelerating throughput of patients. In the ten years 1979 – 1989 the number of available beds per 1,000 population fell from 7.4 to 5.7 while in the number of in-patients rose from 115.6 to 156.8, the average length of stay in acute specialities fell from 9.4 to 6.4 days." [18]

Pressure for the speedy discharge of patients enormously increased and the need for social workers to be on the spot to help them to plan was more apparent. Social workers however were not involved in all instances; some hospitals introduced hospital discharge planners but looked to social workers to handle the most complex situations.

The increased pressure of restricted resources and the consequent need to target them often led SSDs to restructure their management organisation. Despite hard and detailed work on the part of the Principal Officers (Health) it was frequently difficult in these restructuring activities to ensure a considered place for a health-related social work service. The great value of a service based in the NHS, an integral part of its multidisciplinary working and yet part of the local authority service, able to work at the interface between Heath and Social Services, was often obscured, badly supported and indifferently managed. Recognition of the vital contribution made by health-related social workers had to await the introduction of the NHS and Community Care legislation in 1990.

The practice of health-related social work

The great changes in the country's demography and in health care raised one of the major practice issues for health-related social work in this decade. How could the needs of the increasing number of very elderly, frail people be met and answers found to questions raised about their future care? Social workers based in the health service were inevitably involved in the future of these elderly people: they were often unhappy about the ethical issues involved, including the right of elderly people to choose where to live, a right sometimes denied by hospital staff desperate to relieve the pressure on their beds. Social workers found themselves acting as advocates on behalf of the patients and their families, often without much in the way of support or guidance from their higher management, and unconvinced by the new importance given to the private sector.

At the same time health-related social workers had to learn about, and adjust to, working with patients/users who were having new forms of treatment. These often brought ethical dilemmas which had to be confronted by social workers and by those more closely involved with medical care. Advances in transplantation and cardiac surgery, in the survival of very premature babies and the whole field of *in vitro* fertilisation, together with the identification of HIV/AIDS, confronted all social workers, but particularly health-related social workers, with new areas of work.

Many major disasters occurred during the eighties. Hillsborough, Kegworth and Newbury became household names as locations of tragedy. Health-related social workers, together with colleagues in area teams, contributed a great deal to better ways of handling disasters and increased public awareness of the effects of physical and psychological injury. They were able to transfer their knowledge and understanding of individual situations to such events.

Working with people who were acutely ill had always meant that social workers had to come to terms with the thought of death in relation to patients and their families and to themselves. Interest in developing skills in working in what was then known as terminal care, had been evident in the many articles published in the Almoner in the early fifties. Jean Snelling wrote a seminal paper on bereavement and loss, which provided an impetus to carrying this work further. In the sixties many health-based social workers developed specific skills in working with dying people. In the seventies and later, bereavement counselling and groups for bereaved people were often developed in the larger hospitals or in specific units.

Health-related social workers have made a major contribution to the development of the hospice movement. Their specific skills in working with dying people and their families have played a key role. Out of this work the Association of Hospice Social Workers was established in the early years of the 1980s. It offers a network to consolidate and further develop members' work and acts as a reference body in the field of palliative care.

In palliative care, in renal dialysis and in transplantation, social workers regularly take part in multidisciplinary international conferences, an acknowledgement of their valuable contribution to the user's/patient's care and a recognition by the medical profession of their input to health care.

In the 1980s health-related social workers were again active in initiating and facilitating specialist user groups. With the increase in road traffic accidents affecting young people, health-related social workers became involved in setting up brain and spinal injury resource groups such as Headway. In paediatric units, they facilitated groups of parents of premature or disabled babies to meet; continued their work with abused children and worked with children suffering from cancer. In addition they built up expertise in working with families and children who suffer from rare but very distressing and disabling conditions.

Social Work and General Practice

The setting up of the SSDs and the reorganisation of the National Health Service in 1974 made it more possible to provide social work in general practice.

The Seebohm report had stated – *"We regard teamwork between general practitioners and the social services as vital. It is one of our main objectives and the likelihood of providing it is a test we would like to see applied to our proposals for a social service department . . . we wish we could recommend the attachment of a social worker to each of these"* (health centres and group practices).[19]

The Otton report took up this theme from the Seebohm report, devoting a whole chapter to the subject. [20] It summarised the range of functions, identified in studies of experimental attachments, which a social worker attached to a primary health care work team might carry out. The report particularly drew upon the work of Goldberg and Neill who undertook a joint project between the Caversham Group Practice Team (London Borough of Camden) and the National Institute for Social Work Training financed by the City Parochial Foundation. The project covered the five years from 1965 and studied the effect of attaching a social worker to a group practice. At the end of the foreword to the account of the project Dr Hugh Faulkner, General Practitioner, Caversham Centre and Dame Eileen Younghusband, Chairman of the project's Consultative Committee, said – *"Our project was completed before the local authority social service departments came into existence. These comprehensive services can all the better use the excellent pick-up point which a general practice team provides, with its continuing relation to patients unselected in terms of age, sex and class – to quote the Seebohm Report In other words everybody."*[21]

Such early hopes were not followed by any national move to establish close working links between social workers and general practitioners. For not only was there a shortage of qualified social workers, but such attachments need particular skills of negotiation and knowledge of the interrelationship of ill health and social circumstances. There were, however, sporadic developments in the 1970s and 1980s which followed no standard pattern. Most developed from SSD area centres, rather than hospital-based departments, and have varied from full time attachments to once-a-week surgeries. In some rural areas there are more social workers attached to health centres than there are based in the local hospital. As the responsibilities of SSDs increased the incentives for developing work with general practices became more obvious and new approaches have continued.

Research

During this decade health-related social work had a limited presence in social work literature in this country. However, one key research project was carried out by the Scottish Office and published in 1988. Issues such as the users' views of hospital-based social work, and the most valuable place for health/hospital social workers to be based were investigated. The findings of this research concluded that not only was the best service to clients offered from a team based in hospital but that this arrangement also gave the best value for money.

It also showed that:

"At present the hospital social work service in Scotland comprises one in eight of all main grade and one in four of all senior social workers and accounts for over £8 million per annum. Between 1975, when responsibility for this service was transferred from Health Boards to Social Work Departments, and 1981 there was a marked rise in the number of hospital based social workers. In recent years this expansion has continued, but more slowly and less evenly across regions."[22]

Funding new developments

Funding new developments in this decade was not always easy. The local authorities' ability to appoint staff to new areas of work depended upon the funding available, competing demands for social workers, and upon the availability of suitably qualified and experienced staff. New initiatives in health-related social work at this time were most usually financed through joint funding. But as financial restraints became more pressing local authorities were often unwilling to enter into joint finance agreements because of the requirements that they would take up the full cost three (later five) years later.

A health unit's speciality sometimes attracted charitable funds which might be used to employ social workers. Thus it was possible to fund some posts in the MacMillan units (continuing care units or hospices) through joint funding or from voluntary sources, whilst it was not always possible to find the funds to support social workers in the emerging oncology units although those directing the units often requested such a service.

Central government funding on a generous scale was available for social workers and other workers in the new HIV/AIDS services as a part of that developing service.

Charities focusing on specific acute illnesses sometimes felt that to achieve a better service for those patients for whom they were concerned they would offer funds to employ social workers whose work would be dedicated to that field. In particular, the Malcolm Sargent Fund provided social worker posts to ensure that social workers in hospitals are available to children suffering from cancer and their families.

In the field of dialysis and kidney transplantation, patients' demands that they should have access to skilled social work help led the Kidney Patients Association to take the initiative and provide money to establish some new social worker posts.

These specifically funded posts made a particular contribution to the debates about specialisation as they ensured that particular patients received a service and make it possible for social workers in those posts to develop appropriate expertise. They also introduced a new challenge to the management of social workers, as ways had to be found of incorporating workers who had very specific job descriptions and who could not be moved to other parts of the social work agency in which they were based. The mixed economy of welfare had arrived in health-related social work.

Joint funded posts, too, have often been set up through the efforts of those medically responsible for new services, such as a new regional spinal injuries unit. It is perhaps interesting to reflect that all the years of high standard health social work combined with the teaching of medical and nursing students resulted in the effort other professions were willing to put into initiating this kind of post.

Ethnic minorities

The hospital service had been one of the earliest to benefit from immigrant workers, who were encouraged to come to fill many of the posts vacant during the years of full employment. Public transport workers, ward orderlies, cleaners, porters, from different parts of the world became a familiar sight, and an increasing number of ethnic nursing students began to appear on the wards.

The Institute of Medical Social Workers had a long tradition of training students from overseas, most of whom returned home to set up social work departments or to staff existing ones.

Later, immigrants from very deprived areas came in greater numbers and health-related social workers soon realised that extra efforts must be made to cater for their needs. Local authorities could apply for "Section 11" money, to fund extra social work posts to work with clients from minority ethnic groups. Courses were run to enable social workers to learn about and understand the differences in culture which needed to be respected if these new clients were to be given effective help. Hospitals began to employ interpreters and liaison workers to bridge the gap which language problems and lack of knowledge of British institutions could cause.

Hospital-based social workers were much involved in these attempts to offer appropriate help and to lessen the impact of unfamiliar, and possibly frightening, surroundings. Those social workers working with maternity and children's units and in mental health had perhaps the first opportunities to develop and extend this area of work.

Social workers also took an active part in introducing and maintaining practices within health institutions which were more helpful to people from minority ethnic groups. To some extent this has been an extension of the long-standing social work responsibility to represent patients' interests in the health setting. Such initiatives as ensuring suitable interpreters were available at the most critical time, taking the initiative in making it possible for the correct funeral rites to take place and commenting upon local health policy statements to make them "ethnically friendly", were all undertaken by health-based social workers.

Network supports

Some areas of health-related social work remain highly specialised. There was and is a need for support from others in the same field, as demonstrated by the founding of BASW special interest groups. Where social workers were working in a specialised field, this kind of networking offered mutual support, exchange of information and concerted action, maintaining a long-standing tradition in health-related social work. The Association of Hospice Social Workers, for instance, provided one of the main initiatives to bring about improvements in the Attendance Allowance for terminally ill people.

The management of social workers, based in a specialist setting such as the health service, requires specialist knowledge and skills to integrate the service with the setting. For those who are such managers network support can be extremely valuable.

An example of networking to support both social work practice and management of that practice in the health service arose in the early 1980s when the Inter County Group centred on Oxford; a Midlands group centred on Mansfield, and other groups in London and in Scotland came into being. These groups met to discuss the impact of current needs such as those of some elderly people for care, and of the current development of health-related social work. Social work managers in the health service were often very isolated and, especially those new to this form of management, welcomed the mutual support supplied by such useful reference groups. It also offered the opportunity for co-ordinated responses and initiatives.

One such initiative was the Inter-County Group's support of the specialised teaching for health-related social workers centred upon Green College, Oxford. This gap in current training was identified by the Principal Officer in Oxford who had negotiated the setting up of a lecture series offering teaching in aspects of medicine for social workers. It was available to health social workers who were able to travel to Oxford for the day and whose department would support them.

Concern about the need for social workers in health-related fields to have a specialised input into their training led the Inter-County Group to raise funds from the Nuffield Provincial Hospitals Trust to carry through a project to assess this need. The subsequent report of the findings was presented to CCETSW in 1988 to support proposals for a curriculum for the (then) proposed three year qualifying course. This project was followed by another, funded by CCETSW, to examine the area-based social workers' needs for training in health subjects. These reports demonstrated the need for specialised training in health issues for all social workers wherever they might be based. The first had a fairly wide circulation but the second was never published.

In the late eighties a BASW special interest group for health-related social work was set up. The attendance at the first meeting demonstrated that there were many social workers working in the health field, and they were very actively interested in consolidating and developing their area of work.

Education and training

By 1980 the CQSW was well established and the emphasis upon a generic approach to social work meant that training too aimed to offer a generalist approach. An important exception to this might be seen in the post-qualified requirement for Approved Social Workers to have specialist training (1983). Any social worker with two years' post-qualifying experience had to have undertaken special study and, at first, had also to pass an examination set by CCETSW, before they could take action under the mental health legislation. Clearly social workers from a variety of bases might undertake this training and it therefore represented a move to specialist training available to any social worker for whom it was seen as relevant.

At the beginning of this period, the content of training, reflecting the large departments and the desire for a generic approach, often had many subjects added to the core requirements, and professional social work courses were often very crammed. This, together with the effect of the public enquiries in relation to child abuse, led to the proposals for a three-year course. The proposal, however, did not receive government support at that time, although it has continued to be debated.

The government's Training Support Fund which was made available to local authorities was initially directed for use in training in the field of care for the elderly. Later it was seen as an opportunity to increase specialist training especially in residential care and child protection for all grades of worker.

By the end of the decade the CSS was well established. Though highly regarded, especially for its education approach, CSS never attracted the number of students hoped for. Many of those who had gained the certificate had either already continued their training to become qualified social workers or wished to do so. The time had come for a qualification which would embrace both the employment route and the academic route to professional qualification. Thus in 1989 the new Diploma in Social Work (DipSW) replaced both the CQSW and CSS as the professional social work qualification.[23]

Towards the end of the eighties there was also more concern with competence for practice and a recognition that the practice learning element was as important as the academic component in training.[24] Accreditation for practice teaching was introduced. To become accredited practice teachers had to either successfully complete a practice teachers' course or, for those with experience, assemble a portfolio of their work for approval.

In the health field the emphasis in teaching reflected both the legislative requirements and the major priorities of work in the social service area centres. The focus was therefore more upon chronic care than upon the situations of acute illness found in hospital.

Despite this drift away from a specialist focus in education and training, social work in the health field continued to offer a large number of student placements to training courses. In these years student units not only continued in health bases, but were also set up, providing well-structured student experience in social aspects of illness and disability and in working in a multidisciplinary context. The units also provided a dependable standard of supervision offered by practice teachers who had the benefit of the experience of teaching many students.

The social work contribution to medical and nurse education appears to have declined in this decade perhaps due to the pressures of the world of social services and of social work. It may be that where the tradition of such teaching existed and in particular units where the social work contribution was valued in the NHS, it had continued. However, it appears only infrequently in social work literature for this period and would seem to be a real loss as a contribution to greater understanding between the professions. It has to be said, however, that the philosophy taught in earlier decades has borne fruit and many of the human behaviour elements are now incorporated in nurse training.

In social work education and training, the need remains for a more formal requirement for health issues to be included in all basic qualifying courses to meet the needs identified by practising health-based social workers and by the Inter-County projects. This would particularly include learning to work with the human response to acute illness, the onset of disability, and loss; with attention to prevention, rehabilitation, and the organisation of the health services (both public and private).

1990-1995

1990 ushered in a sea change in the practice of social work in the United Kingdom, confirming the trends in social policy of the preceding years. In England and Wales, two major pieces of legislation – the Children Act 1989 and the National Health Service and Community Care Act 1990 – became the cornerstones of SSD activities. The NHS and Community Care Act 1990 also applied to Scotland but the Children (Scotland) Act was only passed in 1995 and circulars and guidance are awaited.

The Children Act changed fundamentally the relationship between children, families and social workers, emphasising not only work in partnership with parents but also parental responsibilities. For the first time, children with disabilities were seen as children with special needs and under Section 17 of the Act became clearly a part of the remit of local authority SSDs. Health-related social workers therefore added work which they had often undertaken in the past to the list of their statutory duties.

The National Health Service and Community Care Act 1990 gave local authorities the responsibility to assess the needs of those seeking care and for making plans to meet the needs identified in partnership with users and carers. Funds for the residential care of elderly people which had been administered by the Department of

Social Security were reallocated to SSDs. Within a multidisciplinary framework, local care managers began to assess need and implement care plans. Emphasis was placed on working with users and their carers and upon flexibility of response. For this to be effective, budgets had to be devolved. SSDs set up financial systems and once again social workers became involved in helping people manage the cost of their care. Discharge planning for people leaving hospital has again become a major activity.

Since SSDs must promote a "mixed economy of care", with 85% of moneys allocated to them under the community care legislation to be spent in the private and voluntary sectors, the nature of the relationships between social workers in each sector has changed, as have their tasks. SSD personnel tend to be purchasers and staff in other sectors providers. Social workers in health settings may be purchasers and providers.

In Northern Ireland, hospital and community health and social services have been organised in separate units of management and new charging arrangements for the hospital social work service have been introduced. The Department of Health and Social Services in its most recent guidance (June 1995) states *"organisational arrangements which promote the continued integration of social work in hospitals within the community social services framework are necessary in meeting quality and standards in relation to patient care".*[25]

The National Health Service

The NHS and Community Care Act also brought major changes to the NHS. The development of trust hospitals posed new issues for health-related social workers. At first many social workers were concerned as to whether as a part of SSDs they could work in trust hospitals. These doubts were dispelled by Department of Health guidance. BASW also responded with a policy statement, The Future of Health Related Social Work (1992)[26] from a working party especially set up to examine the situation.

In general practice the Family Health Service Authorities (FHSAs) were set up, and general practitioners could become fundholders giving them more control over the services which they purchased for their patients and over the type of staff they might employ. The growing trend for general practices to offer a range of services became even more possible. The services of counsellors have often been included in such a range of services, raising issues about key workers where social workers were also in touch with the same doctors and patients. The probability is that social workers attached to practices (as in Wiltshire for example) will find themselves working with people with a complexity of needs including the need for access to other resources. Such social workers will have to have an ability to work closely with a range of other disciplines and have a knowledge of the interrelationship of social and health problems. As in all multidisciplinary situations social workers will also need strong social work support and networks.

Health-related social work

For many years there was little systematic information available about the number, distribution and tasks of social workers in health settings. A Department of Health survey in 1989 estimated that approximately 5,900 health-related staff were employed by local authorities of whom 80% were based in hospitals. The Social Services Inspectorate (SSI) of the Department of Health began a series of inspections. Their report of an inspection of social services for hospital patients in five SSDs "Working at the Interface" was published in 1992,[27] to be followed by a further report in 1992 Social Services for Hospital Patients II: The Implications for Community Care - ". . . *to identify the steps that SSDs need to take with health agencies, to ensure that staff in hospitals are enabled to play a full part in effecting the community care changes".* [28]

The findings of this inspection highlighted the need for social services staff in hospitals to react very quickly and to be *"flexible and decisive to respond effectively in these circumstances".* The importance of multidisciplinary working *"having a distinct not a merged identity"* was noted as was the lead role taken by social workers in adopting a holistic approach to need. Finally it stated that, *"Hospital social work has an important place within the overall provision of social services. The way that it is organised should reflect the objectives of the service rather than be based upon historical accident or traditional beliefs."*

The third inspection studied the users, and carers, perspective, three-quarters of whom found the hospital social service helpful and would use it again. Users and carers found many positive aspects, both practical and in the realm of being good listeners. One user said the social worker gave her *"hope to carry on".*

The NHS and Community Care Act and the inclusion in the Children Act of children with special needs (encompassing children with disabilities) has placed new emphasis upon the importance of health-related social work where it can work as a part of, but distinct from, a multidisciplinary setting. In working with adult people, to be of most help to the user in undertaking assessment at the most crucial time puts the health-related social worker in a key position. Assessment entails detailed examination of the users' and carers' current situation. This may well ensure that aspects are covered that otherwise might have been neglected. However, undue concentration on practicalities runs the risk of excluding their need to talk, be listened to, and to look at solutions for themselves. The value of giving "hope to carry on" cannot be underestimated.

The descriptions given by the users and carers in the SSI report send heartening messages that health-related social work has a great deal of constructive help to offer. Where there is a hospital-based service, the direct access to SSD services envisaged in 1974 works to the user's and carer's benefit.

The Community Care legislation places health-related social work in a key position, assessing the needs of users in a multi-disciplinary context, drawing upon the skills of assessment and multidisciplinary working that have always been at the heart of their work.

In the years 1974-1995 it has often seemed to those social workers involved in it that health-related social work has been obscured. Yet there are more health-related workers now than in 1974. Users and carers value their service often because it is available when need presents itself and the user does not have to seek it out at a time of crisis. Health-related social workers have had to work hard to ensure a visible place in organisations which are more comfortable in focusing the delivery of their services upon area centres. Organisations also have to accommodate the essential nature of health-related social work which is daily involved with issues of illness and death that raise anxieties in us all.

However, no part of social work is without pressure and stress. Each area of work demands that social workers possess the essential knowledge and skill required of that specialism and that they have dependable ways of assessing and handling risk. Risk may relate to users and carers and their physical or mental or emotional capacity to deal with the situations they face. Similar risk may face social workers in their efforts to work with stressed or emotionally disturbed people whose behaviour may be abusive or violent.

Social workers in paediatric care have continued their work in the early detection of child abuse, in the highly specialised area of the acute illnesses of childhood and in working with children with long term disabilities.

Similarly, social workers have continued to develop their work with patients in new areas of medicine. This has also meant integrating their work with medical developments. That this latter task has been accomplished successfully is shown in the respected place they have been given at medical conferences, for example in renal and palliative care.

Equally social work in rehabilitation, acute medicine and surgery, and in care of elderly people has been in areas of work where health-related social work has continued to be a major presence in helping clients/users and their families reach their optimum. The combination of values, knowledge, skill, experience and professional confidence which are particular to a setting, client group or method of working can be seen as producing a social work specialism. This built upon core social work values and skills, resulting in practice of a high standard. The content of such specialisms has certainly changed since 1970 and will continue to change but the essential characteristics will remain.

In 1974 it seemed to many in health-related social work that the skills of health social work practice would be lost. There were certainly major changes, not all of them resulting in better help for the user at the point of need. Becoming a part of large departments seemed often to have the effect of health-related social work being lost to the view of those in higher social services management and area offices. Yet 14 years later Connor and Tibbitt were able to demonstrate clearly their value and almost 20 years later the SSI reported more health-related social workers than in 1974. Perhaps even more importantly the users are quite clear about the value that health-related social work is to them.

Optimum ability to cope.

Both the NHS and Community Care Act and the Children Act emphasise the importance of multidisciplinary assessment, working in partnership and, particularly for adults, the importance of discharge planning. All these are areas of work in which health-related social workers have played a crucial part. After these years of hard work and continuing development health-related social work is once again centre stage.

References
[1] HMSO, Report of the Committee on Local Authority and Allied Social Services, Social Services (HMSO, London, 1968) (Seebohm Report) Cmnd. 3703
[2] CIPFA annual returns and Department of Health and Social Security (DHSS), Health and Personal Social Services Statistics, annual. Quoted in Glastonbury B.,

Cooper D.M., and Hawkins P. Social Work in Conflict: The practitioner and the bureaucrat. British Association of Social Workers 1982

[3] Chronically Sick and Disabled Persons Act 1970

[4] HMSO, Social Work Support for the Health Service, Report of the working party chaired by Mr G.J. Otton. (HMSO, London, 1974) (The Otton Report)

[5] BASW Clients are Fellow Citizens (BASW, 1980). See also Jordan B., Is the Client a Fellow Citizen? Social Work To-day, 2 October 1975

[6] HMSO Better Services for the Mentally Handicapped (HMSO, London, 1971)

[7] HMSO Better Services for the Mentally Ill (HMSO, London, 1975)

[8] HMSO A Happier Old Age, A discussion document on elderly people in our society (HMSO, London, 1978)

[9] CCETSW Social Work: People With Handicaps Need Better Trained Workers (CCETSW Paper 5, London, 1974)

[10] Seebohm Report (1968)

[11] Robinson, John N.G. The Dual Commitment of Social Work, British Journal of Social Work, Volume 2, No.4, 1972

[12] Bartlett H., The Common Base of Social Work Practice, National Association of Social Workers Inc., Washington, D.C. 1970

[13] Otton Report (1974) op. cit. Page 15

[14] Player Alison, Casework in Terminal Illness, The Almoner, Volume 6, No.11, 1954

[15] Pearson Nancy, Casework in Terminal Illness in Great Britain, The Almoner, Volume 6, No.11, 1954

[16] CCETSW, The Certificate in Social Service, A new form of training. CCETSW Paper 9:1, 1975, see also CCETSW Regulations and Guidelines for courses leading to the Certificate in Social Service (CSS) CCETSW, Paper 9:5, 1980

[17] Barclay P. Social Workers: Their Role and Tasks, London, National Institute for Social Work, Bedford Square Press, 1982

[18] Department of Health, Social Services for Hospital Patients 1: Working at the Interface, para 7.9., Social Services Inspectorate, Department of Health, 1992

[19] Seebohm Report (1968) op. cit. para 699

[20] Otton Report (1974) op. cit. Chapter 3, pages 26-30

[21] Goldberg E.M., Neill J.E. Social Work in General Practice, National Institute Social Services Library No. 24, Allen and Unwin, London, 1972

[22] HMSO, Connor A., Tibbitt J. Social Workers and Health Care in Hospitals, Central Research Unit, HMSO, Edinburgh, 1988

[23] CCETSW DipSW: Rules and Requirements for the Diploma in Social Work CCETSW Paper 30, London, 1989, revised 1991, 1995

[24] CCETSW Regulations and Guidance for the Approval of Agencies and the Accreditation and Training of Practice Teachers, CCETSW Paper 26.3, London, 1989

[25] Department of Health and Social Services: Social Services Inspectorate Organisational Standards for Social Work in Hospitals, Belfast, 1995

[26] BASW The Future of Health Related Social Work, British Association of Social Workers, Birmingham, 1992

[27] Department of Health Social Services for Hospital Patients I: Working at the Interface, SSI, 1992

[28] Department of Health Social Services for Hospital Patients II: The Implications for Community Care. SSI., Foreword, 1992

CHAPTER FOUR

1995 ONWARDS – FACING THE FUTURE

Joan Baraclough

As social work moves onwards from this centenary year, what does the future hold? What form of welfare provision will there be before and beyond the millenium? What impact will the economic and social context have on the care of people who are vulnerable through illness or disability?

Will the values which energised the pioneers and sustained their successors continue to influence policy and practice? How will expertise garnered from the cumulative experience of generations of social workers in health and related settings be developed to ensure that people with acute or chronic illness or disability benefit? Can health-related social workers show that what they do makes a difference to people's lives?

Such questions serve as prompts to further action and as reminders of basic principles. There is little doubt that health-related social work is in a strategic position at the interface of health and social care and has a valuable contribution to make to the development of policy and practice of the future. More pertinently, it is evident that users and carers value health-based social work for the difference it makes to their health and well-being.[1]

Basic Principles

1. Social work is a dynamic activity within a social context, with respect for individuals at its core
2. Health is more than health care and is determined by social and economic factors such as nutrition, housing, education, employment, justice and deprivation.
3. Equity of access to health and social care is vital to a healthy society.

Recalling in contemporary language the values and principles from which the first almoners worked, almoners then and social workers now are:

committed to:	putting the patient first
	making cost-effective use of medical and social resources by patient-centred, needs-led, non-judgemental, independent and holistic practice
	promoting partnerships between agencies
informed by:	extensive knowledge of community resources

understanding of the social roots of disease and the impact of illness and

disability on individuals and their carers

awareness and analysis of cultural, economic and psycho-social factors affecting health and well-being

knowledge of helping methodologies.

skilled in: enquiry

needs assessment

planning

advocacy

counselling

promoting independence

maximising service users resources

negotiating

networking

working alongside other professionals [2]

Health-related social work is a many faceted task: often carried out in a host setting; governed by legislation; shaped by its social and economic context; based on professional ethics and education and, most important of all, responsive in micro and macro ways to the needs of service users. Each of these facets will need attention in developing health-related social work for the next century.

Legislative Context

The main planks of recent legislation governing social work, the Children Act 1989 and the NHS and Community Care Act 1990, espouse a caring philosophy, clearly in accord with social work principles. The interest of the child is paramount: children with disabilities are recognised as children with special needs and building partnerships with parents a priority. Patients are to be put first: service users empowered and the needs of both patients and their carers assessed. The legislative context for social work is positive in its regard for individuals and in its emphasis on a holistic approach to patient care, quality services and accountability.

The major contribution made by carers has been recognised: first in the Disabled Persons (Services, Consultation and Repre-sentation) Act 1986, then in the 1990 NHS and Community Care Act and most recently in the Carers (Services and Recognition) Act 1995.

The need to strengthen and improve community services for people with mental health problems was evident even before the introduction of the policy to close large psychiatric hospitals. The latest legislation, the Mental Health (Patients in the Community) Act 1995, is proving controversial with its powers "to take and convey", while recognising the need for supervision powers for those caring for people with severe mental illness after discharge from hospital. This Act illustrates once more the difficult balance that social workers and others have to strike to ensure that protecting one person's rights does not put others at risk. Although legislation to promote equal opportunities and race relations has been on the statute book for some time, it has seldom been seen as relevant in addressing questions of inequalities in health and social care. There are signs that social services and social workers in health settings are giving more attention to this area – a task which is urgent and requires both further training and resources. It is particularly important to ensure that people from black and other ethnic minority groups have timely access to services which recognise their particular culture.

Many of the community care reforms were warmly welcomed. Legislation which enabled people to be looked after in their own homes; envisaged packages of care designed in line with users' needs and preferences and made "proper assessment of need and good care management the cornerstone of high quality care" held great promise of user choice and empowerment. [3]

As legislative provision was translated into services, doubts began to arise, particularly about the long-term care of older people and charging policies. People born since 1945 regarded the Welfare State and its flagship, the National Health Service, as the means of obtaining health and social care for themselves and their families. They were brought up to expect services free at the point of use to meet their needs from cradle to grave. Now they fear moves apparently aimed at limiting the role of the NHS and many aspects of health care being redefined as social care and subject to means testing. Continuing care provision for very old people and for severely disabled people, within the spirit of the 1946 and 1990 NHS legislation, has to be a priority objective for the future. There is a moral imperative to look after the most vulnerable.

There is a need to re-examine the range and balance of provision both in the NHS and in social services so that long- or short-term residential care is available in circumstances where care in the community on a permanent or temporary basis is not a viable option. People experiencing acute episodes of mental illness, those requiring rehabilitation or respite care could then be accommodated as part of their personalised package of care.

The reforms in the health service with the introduction of trusts and fundholding general practitioners are not well understood by the public at large, who see a business culture taking precedence over a therapeutic one.

Though the effectiveness of parts of the 1990 Act is questioned especially when considered in conjunction with social security legislation and fiscal and housing policy, it is clear that the nature of the relationship between health and local authorities has radically changed. Local authorities are giving health issues higher priority on their agendas. The need for collaborative working or partnerships between health and social services is frequently asserted, though while accountability for planning and providing services and structures and funding sources is substantially different in each sector, it is difficult to envisage how this can become a comfortable reality.

By the millenium will there be legislation to put them on the same footing and thus reduce the number of opportunities for tension, confusion and overlap? For many in 1995 it seems that the Welfare State is at a crossroads, possibly soon to go out of business, as economic rather than social considerations dominate the agenda.

Health-related social workers work with service users and carers facing complex and fraught situations at the cutting edge of health and social care. Staff and agencies must continue to contribute their knowledge and experience, gained from practice, to the monitoring and review of legislation.

The Social and Economic Context

Changes in the nature of society are inevitable and seem to have been greater and more frequent in the past decade than in any other since the creation of the Welfare State. Changes in the structure of families have been created by a rising divorce rate, the growth of partnerships, more lone parents and an ageing population. Stress, leading to physical and mental illness, has been engendered by redundancy, mid-life unemployment, limited job mobility and negative equity in the housing market. Poverty, poor housing and fears of discrimination have enhanced feelings of inequality in an increasingly multicultural society.

Terrorism, domestic violence and other forms of aggression and personal abuse add to a sense of insecurity, as does the loss of respect for, or change in, familiar institutions such as the National Health Service. Pride in public service is being eroded; volunteers are becoming harder to find and many charities are experiencing great difficulty in raising funds. The transfer of traditional local authority responsibilities to the private and independent sectors creates anxieties about accountability, standards and effective communication and information systems. There is more questioning of professional expertise and a greater readiness to resort to litigation as more people become able to voice their complaints at the failure of services to meet their own standards. Failures in human relationships exact a heavy price.

The cost of welfare and the proportion of the Gross National Product spent on all the personal social services are clearly a matter of considerable concern, not only to government. The Prime Minister, John Major, has signalled the need to bring about a change of culture so that people begin to think much earlier about making private provision for their retirement and future health and social care.[4]

Social service agencies are concerned about the level of resources available to meet rising need, though the amount spent on services has increased substantially over the years. Efforts to contain the escalating costs of welfare have led to situations where people assessed as in need are left without help. Most social workers accept that rationing systems have to be introduced, while regretting the need for a return of the role of financial gatekeeper.

These trends and the feeling of moving to a more unequal society have been increased by the changes in the National Health Service and a sense of a money-driven, rather than a patient-needs-led, service.

Throughput seems prized above outcome, though there are now signs that more attention will be given in future to evaluating the outcome for users of community care services. This is fundamental for the planning and development of a needs-led service and for the cost effective use of resources. Why otherwise should social workers struggle to provide quality care, within allocated resources, and their managers juggle with budgets in the face of changing local authority and NHS health agendas?

Technical advances in medicine and in other forms of treatment allow help to be given in forms which were not contemplated even a decade ago, but at a price in economic and human terms. Major ethical and moral issues, together with their social consequences, have to be openly debated as new conditions and ways of treating them are tackled.

The well-being of future generations surely requires equity of access to quality services, realistic assessment of need, secure resources and sound financial controls.

The Organisational Context

The history of health-related social work readily demonstrates its capacity to adapt to and absorb the impact of change, while keeping intact its basic principles. Responsiveness to change in its practice environment and to changes in the causation, nature and treatment of illness and in attitudes to health, disease and disability is one of its strengths.

Local government

Social services throughout Great Britain are again in a state of flux and adjustment as preparations are made for the implementation of local government restructuring in April 1996. This will bring changes in the size of authorities; in the spread of their responsibilities and in leadership and team management. Some local authorities will disappear to be replaced by smaller unitary authorities. In other areas, the present two-tier structure of local government will continue.

While supporting in general the philosophy of bringing services more directly under the control of local people, many social workers are troubled about the viability of the smaller unitary authorities and their ability to provide a range of flexible services. This mirrors concern in some counties that the devolvement of budgets to local level has led to fragmentation in the provision of services and inequity of access for service users.

Many staff feel threatened by having to reapply for jobs or anxious and overworked as current tasks are carried out alongside preparations for new responsibilities. Local knowledge and expertise are lost when staff are transferred and working partnerships are disrupted. Such are the generally acknowledged costs of change. Discontinuty for service users and carers is rarely mentioned, though this should be an important consideration.

A growing number of authorities are combining their social services and housing departments, in part as measures of administrative and financial convenience. The importance of good housing to health and well-being has long been recognised. Over a century ago a social worker, Octavia Hill, developed a system of visitors to help people manage their housing problems and avoid debt due to non-payment of rent, and by 1909 Anne Cummins at St Thomas's Hospital had set up a maternity and child welfare clinic to help families with problems of hygiene in the home among other things.

The National Health Service

The NHS and Community Care Act 1990 has brought substantial changes in the structure and organisation of health services. It emphasised the importance of primary care and co-operation with the private sector.

Collaborative working arrangements with social services and increasingly with organisations in the independent sector are being reshaped and re-established, but the lack of coterminosity between the boundaries of health and local authorities continues to be an expensive, inhibiting factor.

In a public lecture as part of the Centenary Year, Denise Platt, Under Secretary for Social Services of the Association of Metropolitan Authorities, called for "a more radical approach to commissioning" and "much closer cooperation between the health commission and social services when planning contract specifications for acute services".[5] Her example, "placing a contract for a number of hip replacements might appear to have nothing to do with social services", illustrates well the need for both health and social services to recognise the impact of illness on service users and the range of component parts their packages of care might require. Greater awareness of the knock-on effects on local authority spending of some NHS decisions about treatment would encourage more efficient use of all public resources and ensure that cost saving in the NHS does not lead to increased costs for local authorities and greater financial pressures on service users. Wider application of such an approach would do much to improve outcomes in both human and financial terms. Is this not an opportunity for health and local authorities to capitalise on the value of partnership for the benefit of service users as well as the public purse?

Health-related social work

The question of payment for the work done by local authority social workers for NHS patients has not been satisfactorily resolved since reorganisation of the NHS and the transfer of NHS social workers to the employment of local authorities in 1974. Local authorities fulfilled their legal responsibilities to provide a service, but often at the expense of quality. Cuts were made in the numbers of staff, especially in London teaching hospitals, to cope with funding shortages and to fill vacancies in other parts of the social services departments. More recently, social workers in hospitals in some areas have been required by their employers only to provide a full service to residents of their own local authority. While such an approach may seem reasonable to an authority accountable for public resources, it is clearly not in the best interests of some patients, with all the overtones of a two-tier service. Further attempts should be made to remedy this situation.

In Northern Ireland new arrangements for charging for hospital social work are being introduced.[6] Items of service are being costed. It will be worth following up the outcomes of this approach. It may also be worth examining the way hospitals and independent practitioners in the United States calculate their charges, though many social workers there would not advocate a replication of their systems.

Given that there is always likely to be a shortfall in resources social workers must become more skilled in providing information about the cost and effectiveness of their work, whether in hospitals or in primary care.

There is increasing evidence that health-related social workers based in hospitals and in the community help to reduce the cost of the care of some NHS patients. By making early contact with individuals, working with them during their treatment and contributing to planning their care on discharge, social workers with specialist knowledge and skill in the health field have proved to be a valuable asset.

A study[7] carried out in 1988 in Scotland found "many examples where lack of hospital social work involvement contributed to unnecessary use of hospital facilities" and in those settings where it was being used effectively "observational data would suggest savings of at least 5% could be due to hospital social work" with greater likelihood of successful discharge arrangements and fewer readmissions. In 1993, the Audit Commission confirmed the essential contribution made by hospital social workers to the provision of seamless services, discharge planning and after-care[8], while SSI reports have shown that hospital patients value contact with on-the-spot social workers.[9]

Now the Department of Health is funding a study being carried out by the Research Unit of the National Institute of Social Work, which will examine among other matters, "the cost implications of social workers and team leaders' use of their time under different arrangements" for work with elderly people and adults with physical disability in both locality based and hospital based teams.[10] If the findings of the study show not only what social workers do with their time and how much it costs, but make comment about the outcomes for patients, it could do much to help clarify some of the current problems caused by the uneven distribution of health-related social workers. The study would be particularly welcome if it can make a contribution to the vexed questions of access to hospital social work for patients who are not residents of the borough providing the service.

It is time that more attention was paid to the way research findings are applied; to the day-to-day experience of social workers and the ways they help users; and to ways in which practice expertise can be developed and the outcomes for users evaluated. Guidance and checklists from government and researchers are useful prompts, but they cannot take the place of the knowledge, understanding and professional judgement of the worker in his/her relationships with users. In highlighting the limitations of checklists in 1975, Lord McCluskey reminded social workers that if you have a checklist of 50 points, it will be the 51st point that is relevant to the situation of the unique individual before you.[11]

Organisational size, structure and procedures for handling issues of management, accountability and quality are recognised as having a significant influence on workers ability to perform effectively. For a time after the 1974 reorganisation of the NHS, health-related social work in some authorities received little consideration as a main-stream social work activity alongside child care, family welfare and mental health. Senior officers were not always sufficiently qualified and experienced in the health field to ensure that the expertise of knowledgeable health-related social workers informed joint planning between health and local authorities or to argue cogently enough for their effective use within the health service.

Implementation of the NHS and Community Care reforms are leading to new modes of organising hospital social work. Some local authorities have retained sizable hospital staff groups, providing services to individuals and groups, through ward attachments. Others have sectorised services by client group, or begun to provide care across the hospital/community divide through teams based in area offices. A few have contracts with voluntary bodies or charities, such as the Malcolm Sargent Fund or the Kidney Patients Association, who fund posts for specific client groups. In the context of empowerment and professional social work, it has been suggested that "the opportunity of employment by health authorities should be restored to social workers, and that social work should be one of the services offered by NHS hospitals and trusts, community health services and general practice".[12] If this proposal is seen as a way of strengthening a holistic approach to patient care and as a means of combating the marginalisation of social work and other contributors, then it should be explored further.

Certainly health-related social workers now identify with social work and would no more wish to be seen as a profession auxiliary to medicine than did the almoners in 1951. In many respects, too much else has changed to make a return to the pre-1972 position, with the problems of access to local authority facilities, a viable proposition. The current climate, with its emphasis on a mixed economy of care and the growth of a contract culture, would seem to give more scope for social workers to become independent practitioners. Social workers could and perhaps should begin to explore new ways of meeting health-related social work needs of individuals, groups and communities, making no assumptions about the continuity of social services in local government.

Organisational standards for social work in hospitals were published in June 1995 by the Social Services Inspectorate of the Northern Ireland Department of Health and Social Services.[13] The department considers that "organisational arrangements which promote the continued integration of social work in hospitals within the community social services framework are necessary in meeting quality and standards in relation to patient care". This is an important statement for several reasons. First, hospital social work is seen as making a major contribution to patient care. Second, hospital social work is clearly identified as part of social services and not marginalised. Third, recognition is given to the importance of standards and quality care. Fourth, setting standards promotes quality and accountability. Fifth, it serves as an encouragement to other parts of the UK to do likewise.

Social work in hospitals was conceived as a remedy for an organisational problem – the overcrowding of the out-patient departments – and began as a response to social need and the efficient use of resources. It endured and remains of strategic importance in fostering good health and social well-being and in bringing patients' needs to the fore. Social workers based in hospitals now, still have to address issues of patients' needs and cost-effective services, but in a highly technical environment, with time to communicate in short supply as in-patient stays shorten. Without time to listen to patients and their carers, time to provide information to enable them to plan and time to work with colleagues, notions of user empowerment and interprofessional collaboration are negated. The same applies to social workers in primary care, in hospices, in voluntary organisations and in social service area teams. Hospital patients suffering the stress and anxiety of acute illness or surgery involving substantial changes to their life-style need and will continue to need the brief and frequent (sometimes daily) communication, care and attention that social workers on the spot can provide. In conjunction with the multidisciplinary team, their task is to help people handle the crises which hospitalisation brings and to assist them to manage their recovery and return to everyday life satisfactorily.

Findings from research sponsored by the Joseph Rowntree Foundation on assessing the social support needs of visually impaired people showed that users and carers wanted both support and information and valued early contact with social workers at the eye hospital.[14] Certification and registration are a significant and often disturbing experience for visually impaired people and their supporters. Workers need to be sensitive to the impact of being told that one's sight has irrevocably deteriorated. One father who found contact with the social worker very constructive commented: "Although he [his son] must have known it, to be actually told . . . it really does hurt."

Expertise in handling crises, individual and communal disasters, bereavement and loss derives from the application of the basic knowledge and skills of health-related social work.

Primary care

General practices and health centres are productive locations for dealing with social problems. Service users comment that there is no stigma attached to seeing a social worker in a clinic. It provides the opportunity for all aspects of care to be considered together and possibilities for broadening the skill mix of staff. Although social work was introduced to general practice in 1947 and a series of studies from then onwards have pointed to its value, financial constraints and a shortage of appropriately qualified staff inhibited its development. Now a growing number of social workers are working to good effect in general practices and see them as having the greatest potential for meeting the health-related social work needs of services users. Given shorter hospital stays and more care in the community, primary care would seem a major area for the investment of health-related social work skills in the future.

Voluntary organisations continue to make a major contribution to the development of social services for people with specific medical and psychiatric conditions. Recently the Family Welfare Association (formerly the Charity Organisation Society) has been working with general practitioners in some London boroughs to provide counselling and social work services.[15]

Such developments are to be welcomed, but further attention should also be given to the continuing unevenness of access to health-related social work. Though no one would imagine that every person admitted to hospital or seeing a doctor needs social work help, accumulating experience suggests that the numbers who could benefit if services were more widely available have been seriously underestimated. The present shortage of general practitioners adds to the case for multidisciplinary health and social primary care.

Further evidence of the impact of recent policy changes should emerge from another NISW project which is evaluating community care arrangements for older people with dementia.[16]

Anxieties that the most vulnerable people or "difficult cases" may be left unprovided for as the mixed economy of care gives way to increased monopolistic privatisation are increased by the limited attention given to prevention and rehabilitation, and in the case of mental illness to recognition and treatment of symptoms at an early stage.

Facilities for short term care will continue to be needed for assessment and care planning and to give individuals and their families respite from the continuing and exhausting tasks involved providing long term care.

Support for those being cared for at home will also need further attention, as the supply of those able to care diminishes. Families and other carers, old and young, will continue to provide the bulk of care for older people, for those with special needs and for those who live with long or short term disability. In doing so, some endanger their own health or prospects or run the risk of exploitation. Children who care are perhaps the most vulnerable. Here again attention to prevention should pay dividends. Identification of risk factors, awareness of critical points and timely intervention are part of the social work repertoire which should be applied to carers' needs too.

Where local authorities have a range of health facilities attracting patients who are non-residents, there are concerns that a two tier service might develop. Already there are examples of patients receiving minimum help and being referred back to their own area in ways which do not promote continuity of care.

The Professional Context

Over the past two decades the image of social work has not been good, despite an increasing place in legislation. However, there are now small signs that the profession is growing again in public esteem. Understanding of the problems, pressures, stress and sometimes violence suffered by social workers in the course of their work is more evident. Social workers themselves have begun to articulate more clearly what they are trying to do: through their practice and through their contributions to debates on public issues and on the development of their profession.

Health-related social work was described by one county councillor during the centenary year[17] as the unsung and very often unseen section of social services, yet it made a vital contribution to the health and well-being of members of the community. This compliment highlights one of the issues which social workers must face. To promote the development of the profession, new forms of communication have to be developed to show what social workers do, what principles and standards they uphold and how effective their work is. To advance public undertanding of the work, the messages must be clear and readily understood.

Health-related social work is a specialism within social work which can be practised in a number of settings. Throughout their history, almoners, then medical social workers and now health-related social workers have been at pains to maintain their social work identity and uphold its values and principles. This was made evident by the change of name in 1964 and in 1970 by the closure of the Institute of Medical Social Workers once the new, unified social work organisation, the British Association of Social Workers, was established. This was reaffirmed by their adoption of the "main skills from the same base" principle and their transfer to local authority social service/social work departments. There was never any doubt about their belief that social work could and should make a major contribution to health care, nor that social work expertise developed in the health field was transferable and applicable in other settings.

"Having come late to [local authority] social services" as Denise Platt put it[18], hospital social workers found themselves working at the interface of two major services and in some respects marginalised by both. The resurgence of interest in what is now known as health-related social work came with discussions in preparation for the NHS and Community Care legislation. Social workers, some of whom had no previous experience or specialist training in this field, began developing new ways of providing services.

In looking to the future it is essential that the social work practice, management and organisational skills of a wider group are applied to the tasks of providing services, developing interagency collaboration and promoting health. It will be as important to tackle the social conditions which undermine well-being as to provide services to people who are ill. In such a scenario, health-related social work would become a core business. Specialist knowledge and skills would be used and developed and the current frustrations among some practitioners that the essential elements of practice are being crowded out by the volume and administrative nature of the work would be reduced.

Working together in the community

The care in the community philosophy has encouraged a revival of interest in primary care. Social workers recognise the value of working alongside colleagues from other disciplines providing services to the same user. With more people being treated in the community, even when surgery is required, work in general practice could prove professionally satisfying and cost effective. The role and tasks of all members of the primary care team would bear re-examination and redefinition to clarify the specialist and overlapping functions. Having a social worker in post would certainly not mean that only the social worker saw people with social and emotional problems; nor would it mean that he or she only provided information and practical services. The social worker's essential task will continue to be a combination of counselling and social care planning. For the future it will be necessary to find a comfortable balance between social action and social casework if the philosophy of current legislation is to be truly effective. Empowering service users means enabling them to help themselves – social casework, while involving service users in planning, means developing new partnerships in social action.

Counselling is a good example of a term in common use, but conveying different meanings to different people. Counselling is a way of talking over with people in a professional and positive way whatever is troubling them. It is an approach that can be used by many disciplines. In the health field it is perhaps an indication of the growth of the holistic approach to health care that many more health professionals undertake their own kind of counselling. It has become important to know about the person as well as the disease. Social workers' previous experience of contributing to the professional education and practice of other disciplines leads them to see merit in reviving opportunities for interprofessional consideration of the differences and similarities in the objectives and methods of counselling.

Maintaining professional standards

Counselling is also a good example of an issue which is, and will continue to be, of public and professional concern – namely how to establish and assess competence and its counterpart, how to regulate and eliminate bad practice as part of a process of protecting vulnerable people.

From the earliest days, standard setting and the regulation of the profession were tasks undertaken by social workers themselves through their professional bodies. Their councils, which in the case of almoners and later psychiatric social workers, contained a number of distinguished non-social workers, set high standards for practice and education, approving courses of training and only admitting to their professional registers those who successfully completed an approved course. Only those on the registers were eligible for employment and payment as fully qualified social workers in the NHS, a position which continued until 1974. The disciplinary boards were rarely required to act. The preferred course of action for dealing with bad practice was through staff supervision, the provision of training and employer sanctions.

None-the-less, as social work and social services expanded and diversified: first the Association of Social Workers in 1955 and, at regular intervals during the next four decades, BASW and others have put forward proposals for a regulatory body. There is now greater consensus among interested parties about the value of such a development and the government has promised to issue a consultation paper outlining proposals for the establishment of a General Social Services Council.[19]

Alongside the need for a General Council is one for a strong professional association, which can truly hear and encompass a wide range of views in constructive ways. A professional body should be the guardian of professional values and of professional expertise, much as individual social workers should take responsibility for the competence of their practice and professional development.

Since its inception, the British Association of Social Workers has consistently promoted high standards of practice, defining and redefining a code of ethics for social workers and advocating the empowerment of service users. BASW currently has some 8,000 members, a proportion of the workforce similar to that in other professions, but far short of its potential. One urgent task for the future is to promote and develop a broad and active membership, emphasising collaborative effort and recognising the parallel but different role of trade unions.

The history of medical and psychiatric social work demonstrates the value and effectiveness of professional peer group support through a strong professional body and outside the employing agency. In 1991 BASW established the Health Related Social Work Special Interest Group to provide a forum for all those working in the field to identify key problems confronting practitioners, and to promote more effective practice, thus complementing the work of the standing committees. There was a very positive response from social workers.

Writing about the strategic importance of hospital social work, Eileen McLeod concludes that "there is growing evidence that hospital social work [and social workers in GP practices and hospices] can make an important contribution to a more equitable experience of health" and "developments in the local authority sector, which are still in their infancy, together with the growing assertiveness among hospital social workers, offer the best guarantee of hospital social work realising its potential".[20]

Such evidence of assertiveness and preparedness to be analytical and responsive to change is important for "social workers must confront and discharge their own responsibilities for the future of their occupation. If they don't care about it, why should anyone else?"[21]

Assessment, always central to social work practice, and a key component in the development of community care, is also of importance in the development of the profession. Assessment of the need for health-related social work and of the quality of practice would clarify how social workers help and what makes a difference to users. The key to future development must lie with the human resources: professionals readily available to provide the services; well-informed, well-adjusted, well-educated, well-supported people from a range of backgrounds, well attuned to the needs of vulnerable people in a diverse, changing multicultural society.

The Educational Context

One of the hallmarks of health-related social work during the past 100 years has been the emphasis on the importance of education and training. Interference in the lives of vulnerable people, as Sir Charles Loch put it then, demands an educated mind and practical experience. These characteristics have laid an enduring foundation for social work education and will continue to be valid.

As with social work, education and training have to be responsive to the requirements of their time. In the past decade changes in the form and content have been substantial, while the values and essence of the work still stand. The six core competences which those hoping to qualify for the Diploma in Social Work must demonstrate are:

communicate, engage and promote
enable
assess and plan
intervene
work in organisations
develop professional competence[22]

Choice and flexibility in the form of training and in subsequent practice are catered for by a system of general and particular pathways and access is encouraged by the availability of a range of patterns. The general statements appear to cover the requirements for effective health-related social work apart from knowledge of the setting. Monitoring and review in due course will be useful tests of the outcome of change.

The introduction of national vocational qualifications and arrangements for post-qualifying study, leading to advanced and higher awards in social work, has been welcomed as extending the range of continuing education opportunity for all grades of worker. Perhaps more than ever before, the pace of change demands that all professionals maintain and develop their skills by means of continuing education throughout their professional lifetime.

Efforts to introduce three year qualifying courses in social work, in line with other countries in the European Community, have not yet been successful, despite the debates in the House of Lords introduced by Baroness Faithfull and reports of conferences such as that promoted by the Sieff Foundation. The issue should be pursued, in the interest of quality care for service users.

Practice learning has always been a compulsory part of social work courses. Energy, commitment and resources are needed to cultivate and expand practice learning opportunities in hospitals, primary care and other health settings. This would be valuable for several reasons. First, a very substantial number of referrals with a health component are made to social services departments. Second, good collaboration between health and local authority personnel is essential to quality care for service users. Third, the development of multiprofessional training at all levels and especially at higher degree level, adds to mutual professional understanding. Fourth, health settings are fertile ground for gaining experience of the impact of illness, causation, treatment and related social problems. Fifth, service users may be of any age, any class, any religion or any ethnic group and require relevant responses. Sixth, health settings provide knowledge and experience of complex organisations. Seventh, the maintenance of health-related social work calls for a continuing supply of experienced and well-trained personnel.

Recognition of the need for further education and training qualifications for specific areas of work, begun with approved social workers, has continued with the accreditation of practice teachers. There is pressure for similar arrangements for social workers involved in working with abused children and for those responsible for providing professional guidance and support on complex cases for colleagues. One way of progressing this would be to extend the career ladder for practitioners, so that social workers, like other professionals, especially in the health field, could if they wished continue in direct work with service users for their professional lifetime, without being penalised in terms of seniority. A change in grading would provide an added incentive to undertake training.

The growth of private health and social care services provides scope for the appointment of independent practitioners. How well the education and training systems cater for the needs of independent social work practitioners would bear examination. Social workers wishing to undertake post-qualifying programmes already have difficulty in obtaining support for fees and daily living, though some employers allow time for study. Comparisons with the ways in which continuing education for doctors and nurses is funded show social workers are at a disadvantage, especially on multi-disciplinary courses. Ways need to be found to remove such constraint on the development of collaborative services in education.

Another, and more serious, constraint on the development of high quality services is the management capacity of agencies. Frequently management is construed in terms of buildings and finance and rarely in terms of human resources. Yet people – staff – are an agency's most valuable asset. In what ways will CCETSW and/or the lead industry body, the Social Care Consortium, promote training for personnel management? Staff support and supervision, which in social work are a professional activity, may be regarded by some non-professionals as unnecessary, though they have the same purpose as seeking a second professional opinion in medical and legal circles. There is surely an onus on managers at all levels, as on social workers, to acquire the basic professional competences for their tasks.

A further group, social work academics, make a vital contribution through teaching and research to the quality of social work. Their input to practice through thinking, discussion, research and writing is very necessary to succour a profession which, in working with human beings, should never be mechanistic. Health-related social work has been greatly enriched over the years by a long line of distinguished teachers.

With the closure of specialist courses and the reduction in specialist teaching posts, measures need to be taken to ensure that the knowledge base of health-related social work is maintained and developed. These might include: attention to the image of social work in universities; closer collaboration with educators in related services; continuing education for academics in the form of opportunities to engage in practice as well as in research or to develop teaching skills and promotion of the cost effectiveness of social work education. Initiative and innovation need to be encouraged in the face of financial constraints in universities. The development of a well-trained work force for health-related social work should be a major target for CCETSW and all other bodies concerned with social work education, as it must be also for agencies and the profession itself. A training strategy for the personal social services based on a competence approach and the objective of a fully qualified work force is surely in the best interests of service users.

The International Context

Health-related social work is a world-wide activity. Many countries looked to the United Kingdom or the United States of America for guidance in developing their provision. Dr Richard Cabot appointed a social worker (almoner) at Boston General Hospital in 1905 after seeing Miss Cummins's work at St Thomas's Hospital. Miss Agnes McIntyre, deputy almoner at St Thomas's, went to Melbourne, Australia in 1929 and set up that country's first almoner service. Miss Lyall went to Cyprus and Miss Thompson to Palestine to help to develop provision in those countries.

In 1995 to mark the centenary of health-related social work, social workers in Australia, Ireland, India and Norway have held special events and reviewed their origins and achievements. Social workers who trained in the UK but now work or live in France, Germany, Canada, Hong Kong and the USA, to mention but a few, attended events here. Meanwhile in January, in Jerusalem, the first post-war international conference on Social Work in Health and Mental Health was held, with 600 participants from 26 countries. It is predicted that the second conference to be held in January 1998 in Melbourne, Australia will attract even wider representation.

It is striking that despite social, cultural and economic differences, the core values underpinning health-related social work world-wide are remarkably similar. Seeing your own country through another's eyes can provide a productive and sometimes unexpected perspective on what is, and on what needs, to be done.

Around the world, while there are signs of change in the way health care is being provided, there is greater recognition of the need for health-related social work. The message given by the Norwegians on their poster: *Better health with social work in hospitals* [and other health settings] is an encouraging message for us all.

Conclusion

Health-related social work is in a strategic position to influence the development of both health and local authority services. The re-emergence of groups concerned for people coping with the impact of illness; for quality services and inequalities in provision; ready to examine practice and contribute to research; endeavouring to expand education and training and giving attention to communication and collaboration, bodes well for the future. By grasping current opportunities health-related social workers can rightly say they are contributing positively to the legacy for those that succeed them in the future.

Postscript

The preceding chapters have drawn attention to many of the significant events and issues of the past 100 years of health-related social work. They have indicated the substantial changes which have taken place in society and in social work since the appointment of the first almoner in 1895.

During the Centenary Year many tributes have been paid by ministers, civic leaders, heads of professions and above all users and carers, to the valuable and usually unsung work of social workers.

Whether in health-related social work or in other settings, they have been seen as "making a difference".

This account of the history of health-related social work is intended as a tribute to all users and carers – the reason for our being – and as a background for future health-related social workers as they continue to provide and develop services with sick and disabled people.

References
[1] SSI: Social Services for Hospital Patients III: Users' and Carers' Perspective, Department of Health, 1993
[2] Developed from the BASW Briefing Paper for the Parliamentary Reception, 1995
[3] Department of Health, Caring for People, HMSO, 1990
[4] The Times, 14.9.95
[5] Platt, D., A Centenary of Health Related Social Work: Then, Now and Onwards, BASW, 1995
[6] DHSS/NI, Management Executive, New Charging Arrangements 1995
[7] Connor, A. and Tibbitt, J. E., Social Workers and Health Care in Hospitals, HMSO, 1988
[8] Audit Commission, Taking Care: Progress with Care in the Community, HMSO, 1993
[9] SSI, op. cit.
[10] Levin, E. Moriarty, J. Pahl, J. and Webb, S. Social Work and Community Care, National Institute for Social Work, 1994
[11] McCluskey, Lord, Annual General Meeting, BASW, Edinburgh, 1975
[12] Utting, W. B., Empowerment and Professional Social Work, Hertfordshire County Council Social Services, 1993
[13] SSI, Organisational Standards for Social Work in Hospitals, Department of Health and Social Services, Belfast, 1995
[14] Lovelock, R. and Powell, J., Shared Territory: Assessing the social support needs of visually impaired people, Joseph Rowntree Foundation, 1995
[15] FWA, Family Welfare Association's Service Profile, 1995
[16] Moriarty, J. et al. Arrangements for older people with dementia, NISW, 1994
[17] Unpublished speech, Hertfordshire County Council centenary event, 1995
[18] Platt, D. op. cit.
[19] Professional Social Work, February, 1996
[20] McLeod, E. The Strategic Importance of Hospital Social Work, Social Work and Social Sciences Review, 6 (1) 1995
[21] Utting, W. B., op. cit.
[22] CCETSW, Review of the Diploma in Social Work, Final Consultation Papers, November, 1994

A HUNDRED YEARS OF
HEALTH-RELATED SOCIAL WORK

1869 Charity Organisation Society or COS (now the Family Welfare Association) formed to co-ordinate charitable giving and help those most able to use support, using assessment and clear principles.

1892 House of Lords select committee on the abuse of hospitals in the metropolis recommends the appointment of almoners as a means of controlling overcrowding in out-patient departments and the abuse of free hospital treatment by those who can afford to pay.

1895 Mary Stewart the first almoner is seconded by COS to the Royal Free Hospital in London to set up the hospital social service.

1898 Helen Nussey appointed first almoner at Westminster Hospital.
Edith Mudd appointed almoner at St George's Hospital.

1901 Queen Victoria dies.

1902 Thomas Cramp. First male almoner – appointed to Metropolitan Hospital, London after in-service training at the Royal Free Hospital under Miss Brimmell.

1903 Hospital Almoners Committee formed to discuss "the difficulties and possibilities of the work".

1905 Anne Cummins appointed first almoner at St Thomas's Hospital.

1907 Hospital Almoners Council formed to oversee training and recruitment of almoners.
Ida Cannon from Boston, Massachusetts visits London to discuss mother and child welfare.

1910 Edith Mudd moves to Leeds to establish the service there.

1912 Certificates awarded by the London School of Economics for training as almoners or assistant almoners.

1914- First World War. British Red Cross Society and Order of St
1918 John offer scholarships to any of their Voluntary Aid Detachment who wish to train as almoners.

1922 The Hospital Almoners Association formed with 51 members.

1924 Medical Research Council appoints almoner to its Children's Committee.

1928 First International Conference of Social Workers in Paris. Commonwealth Fund of America enables UK almoners to go to USA to study "psychological work" with children. Child guidance services develop.

1929 Mental Health Course founded at London School of Economics under Sybil Clement Brown. Agnes Macintyre from St Thomas's Hospital appointed almoner at the Royal Hospital, Melbourne – the first in Australia.

1930 Association of Psychiatric Social Workers established.

1939-

1945 Second World War.

1940 Emergency Medical Service confirms need for almoners. Ministry of Labour classifies almoners' posts as reserved occupations.

1941 Beveridge Committee set up. Hospital Almoners Association submits evidence.

1945 The HAA and the Institute of Hospital Almoners combine to form the Institute of Almoners. Register of qualified almoners set up. Minister of Health recommends that hospitals employ only qualified almoners.

1948 National Health Service set up. Almoners, freed from task of assessing patients' capacity to pay, concentrate on doing social work. Jane Paterson, in Edinburgh, first almoner to work in general practice.

1950s Flowering of analytically based casework, with emphasis on careful assessment of family dynamics and what each could offer in deciding how help could best be given.

1951 The Cope Committee on Medical Auxiliaries says almoners are engaged in tasks which are an essential element of hospital services. The Institute builds on the committee's recognition of social work as an independent profession, not one auxiliary to medicine.

1954 First University Course in Medical Social Work founded at Edinburgh University. Applied Social Studies Course began at London School of Economics.

1959 Mental Health Act. The working party on social workers in the local authority health and welfare services, chaired by Dame Eileen Younghusband, recommends a new two year training course, with supervised fieldwork for half the time.

1960s Concern grows as increased evidence of baby battering is uncovered.

1960s Medical social workers contribute to developing knowledge and skill in work with children admitted to hospitals and their families.

1962 The Health Visiting and Social Work (Training) Act leads to the Council for Training in Social Work being set up to oversee training for staff in local authority health and welfare departments.

1964 The Institute of Almoners changes its name to the Institute of Medical Social Workers

The Kilbrandon Committee on juvenile delinquency recommends the setting up of juvenile panels and a comprehensive family service within the education department.

1968 The Social Work (Scotland) Act locates services in new social work departments led by directors who are qualified social workers.

The Seebohm Committee on local authority and allied personal social services recommends a new local authority department to provide a community based and family orientated service.

1970 Chronically Sick and Disabled Persons Act.

The Local Authority Social Services Act unifies personal social services in England and Wales in new social services departments.

BASW is formed from seven organisations of social workers.

1971 CCETSW set up, with responsibility for training all social workers in UK.

Certificate of Qualification in Social Work established.

1973 NHS Reorganisation Act provides for the transfer of NHS social workers to local authority departments and medical and nursing staff from local government service to the NHS.

In Northern Ireland four Health and Social Service Boards became accountable for providing integrated health and social services throughout the province.

Mary Windsor, almoner, later Principal Officer (Health), Westminster, first British social worker to become President of the International Federation of Social Workers and to serve two terms.

1974 NHS social workers in England and Wales become employees of the local authority but remain based in health settings.

Arrangements for social work support set out in the Otton Report.

1975 NHS social workers in Scotland transfer to local authority employment but remain placed in health settings.

Arrangements for health-related social work set out in Mitchell Report.

Certificate – Social Service pilot schemes set up.

1979 The Royal Commission on the National Health Service studies criticisms of the new arrangements but concludes "those involved should have the appropriate training and sufficient authority to carry out the task". It adds "the provision of social work services is essential to good patient care".

1980s Health-related social work develops work with patients undergoing new forms of treatment, increasingly working in partnership with others – particularly service users.

1982 The Barclay working party concludes that it would be premature to set up a General Social Work Council as a means of developing and maintaining standards. It urges steps should be taken to formalise clients' rights.

1983 Mental Health Act legislates for "Approved Social Workers".

1984 Data Protection Act gives individuals right of access to personal data and results in social workers giving greater attention to quality of records.

1986 Disabled Persons (Services, Consultation and Representation) Act provides for assessment and carer and user participation.

1988 Connor and Tibbitt in "Social Work and Health Care in Hospitals" demonstrate the cost effectiveness of social workers based in hospitals.

1989 The Children Act includes provisions relating to children with disabilities.

Diploma in Social Work replaces both CQSW and CSS.

NVQ introduced for staff in social services.

1990 NHS and Community Care Act stresses the need for partnership between services and with service users. A key element is the need for assessment and care planning for hospital discharge.

1992 The Social Services Inspectorate issues three reports on Social Services for hospital patients.

1993 SSI Chief Inspector's third annual report illustrates the extent to which users of local authority social services are people with health problems – most adults and some children. The challenges of elder abuse, child abuse, assessment, and hospital discharge planning staff who understand health conditions and have the capacity to work collaboratively, it says.

1994 Post Qualifying and Advanced Awards in Social Work introduced.

1995 SSI (Northern Ireland) publishes guidance on "Organisational Standards for Social Work in Hospitals".
BASW and other agencies hold events to mark the Centenary of Health-Related Social Work.

HOSPITAL SOCIAL WORK IN WARTIME

Doris M. Thornton

On the outbreak of war in September 1939 a state of national emergency was declared, and the Emergency Medical Service (EMS) came into force. Clinics were closed and for a brief period normal admissions were suspended. Most of the larger hospitals in inner-city areas became "sector headquarters", with a network of first aid posts, casualty clearing stations and base hospitals outside the cities. They had a fleet of ambulances and messengers and out-riders on motor bicycles to move quickly around the sector.

The government had, however, underestimated the needs of people living and working in the cities, and acutely ill patients continued to arrive, although they had to be admitted through the casualty departments. Wartime conditions led to a number of admissions, especially road accidents and falls due to the blackout. The stresses of war also took their toll of the more vulnerable. For example, on the night when the news of the sinking of the Ark Royal was released, 17 attempted suicides were admitted to one London hospital. Many of them were refugees convinced that the horrors of Nazi Germany from which they had fled would now overtake them in England.

By 1940 the bombing of London and other cities such as Bristol, Liverpool and Coventry had begun and many almoners lived in their hospitals because of the difficulty of travelling, but chiefly because so much enemy action took place at night. The first aid posts treated the walking wounded, although many of them were subsequently brought to hospital. The seriously injured came straight to hospital. Those too ill to travel were kept in, but as many casualties as possible were transferred to base hospitals for their own safety, and to free beds for the next night's casualties. Each morning Green Line buses, converted into ambulances, drew up outside the hospital. They were driven by young service women who skilfully manoeuvred their heavy vehicles round bomb craters and rubble.

On arrival at hospital every patient was given an "MPC 47". This vital wartime document was a large brown envelope with all the identifying information on the outside, and inside all the medical notes, X-rays and other relevant information which would be helpful to the receiving hospital. Wherever they went the MCP47 travelled with patients, who sometimes had to be moved on from the base hospital to special centres, such as a burns unit or orthopaedic hospital.

Old barriers and lines of demarcation were broken down in wartime, and the MPC47 was completed by whoever saw the patient first – doctor, nurse or almoner. The important thing was to identify patients as quickly as possible, with the help of ambulance drivers or civil defence workers if friends or relatives were not with them.

The needs of the patient were manifold but the most urgent was overwhelming anxiety about relatives and friends. One woman who had severe head injuries, for example, refused to stay on the stretcher taking her to the theatre until she had news of her four-year-old son. She had remarried and the little boy's name was different to hers (he was, in fact, already in another operating theatre in the hospital having surgery for a shattered kneecap). Other needs were more symbolic – like that of the elderly lady, carried out of the wreckage of her home, who next morning firmly refused to be put into the Green Line ambulance until she had been provided with a clean pocket handkerchief. . . .

As the war progressed, more and more "categories" of patients were accepted as eligible for treatment under the EMS arrangements – Land Girls, transferred munitions workers, the Bevin boys from the mines. But there were those who did not fit into any of the specified categories and who were sometimes difficult to place. One night during a particularly heavy air raid a baby boy of about 10 months of age was handed out of an ambulance. He was wrapped in an army blanket and described by the ambulance crew as "a blooming miracle" because he was found in a bombed house – its only survivor. "Not a scratch on him", said the doctor, "bed him down for the night, then get him out of here."

At 8 o'clock the next morning a request to sector headquarters to arrange to take him in the convoy leaving London met with refusal because the baby was not a casualty. Nor did the LCC Welfare Department take kindly to the request to admit to institutional care a baby without a name or date of birth, and who may or may not have been vaccinated and immunised against whooping cough and measles. But even worse was that he had no next of kin. "You know perfectly well that we do not evacuate unaccompanied children under three years", was the response to the almoner. Much of the rest of her day was spent climbing up the ladder of municipal authority until, at 5pm, a place was found for him. An illegal ride in an ambulance took him to Liverpool Street Station just as the sirens were sounding, plunging the whole station into darkness. It was 9pm when the almoner handed him over to a warm welcome at the end of the journey.

The medical and nursing staff who had been transferred to the institutions that had been converted into base hospitals were appalled at the conditions they sometimes found when they arrived. Gradually, however, conditions improved as, one by one, wards were upgraded and essential equipment was brought in. Almoners (often the young and newly qualified) were appointed to help patients, many of whom were homeless, bereaved, and sometimes with injuries needing long-term treatment.

Their main difficulty often lay in the attitude of the administrators of these institutions who saw no reason why an almoner should need an office, or a telephone or clerical help. The feeling was that, as she only had to talk to patients, she could do that on the wards. Urged by the professional association, the Ministry of Health agreed to create special senior posts as Regional Almoners. Their job was to pioneer the new posts in the base hospitals, using their seniority and experience to smooth the way for younger colleagues. As one such Regional Almoner, in lighter mood, described her role:

> I'm the starter-up of new jobs
> The girl who gets things done
> From Peru to Timbuktu jobs
> Are waiting to be won.
>
> Through water-tight compartments
> I permeate by charm
> Setting up departments
> And guarding them from harm
>
> And when an erring hospital
> Has reached a state of grace
> A gently *lady* almoner
> Can come and take my place

> (Helen Bate)

By 1941 the news of civilian casualties and bombed homes had touched the warm hearts of the women of America, who responded with "bundles for Britain". Great tea chests full of clothing began to arrive at hospitals in the bombed areas. The contents of these chests, while not severely practical, were a wonderful tonic in the drab days of wartime utility. Little boys on crutches wore cowboy suits from the Mid-West, babies appeared in bright pink and blue layettes from the southern states; while from New York came sequinned dresses and fur coats. There was a certain satisfaction in being able to wrap a battered and shivering old lady from an East London street in American mink.

The experiences of the war years brought about a great change in attitudes. It was reflected not only in the spate of reforming legislation but in the changes these led to in social policies and in social work. It can be argued that the notion of community care had its beginning in the bringing together of civil defence workers, police, British Red Cross, the clergy and many others who were working together to unite families and to help them to rebuild their shattered lives. It meant that almoners, too, found themselves working with the wider community, and reaching out far more beyond the walls of the hospital.

Within the hospital, the recognition of the almoner as a member of the medical team was also strengthened. Increasingly, almoners were included in the process of diagnosis and treatment of patients. Because doctors' perception of what almoners could offer had been sharpened by the war years, referrals came less often as a prescription the doctor ordered, and more often as a request along the lines of "I cannot do a thing about her arthritis. Can you do anything about her loneliness?"

Perhaps greatest of all the changes in attitude was that towards people with disabilities. For these, the acute shortage of labour during the war resulted in new employment opportunities. Men and women who were, on medical grounds, excluded from the armed forces were eagerly recruited for work in which dexterity and skill were more important than physical strength. Many who became a valued part of the workforce were able to enjoy a new-found financial independence and the camaraderie of their fellow workers. Their right to employment was confirmed by the passing of the Disabled Persons (Employment) Act 1944. As a result, almoners were often invited to take part in training courses for the disablement resettlement officers, and to sit on the local Disablement Advisory Committees that were established under the Act.

In 1943 the Medical Research Council (MRC) carried out a survey on patients with non-static disabilities. It had already established that blind people and those who had suffered amputations could be placed in work with few problems. It was more difficult to find sympathetic employers for those with less visible disabilities or fluctuating health. The research was carried out from the cardiac department of the London Hospital, where the MRC partly funded the salary of the almoner because it was recognised that many of the patients needed practical help and social support before they could face the problems of getting back to work.

After a year the survey was widened to include children with disabilities, many of whom were attending special schools. It was found that the gentle regime of lessons interspersed with periods of rest and handicrafts did little to equip these children to earn their own living. The survey confirmed that poor education was the chief reason why school-leavers found it hard to find suitable work. As a result of representations made to the Ministry of Education by the paediatric almoners' group, a clause was inserted into the Education Act 1944. It stated that no child by reason of a physical disability should be denied the education from which intellectually he was able to benefit. It was this change that was to open the doors to higher education for those with disabilities.

Essex 1995

SOCIAL WORK IN 1945

Diana Glover

Somehow it did not seem as though we were approaching a victorious end to the war. In January 1945, even in London, there was deep snow, frozen pipes and no coal. The hospital was warm and brightly lit as, on the 8th of January, 35 air raid casualties were admitted with four children huddled together in one bed and after treatment 21 people waiting to be reunited with their families or going on to a Rest Centre. Air raid warnings continued day and night and whereas the earlier Blitz had been noisy with "friendly" anti-aircraft fire, the V1 flying bomb and V2 rocket now falling on London were deadly and virtually unopposed with only the drone of the former and the silence following the engine cut-out before the inevitable explosion. Patients on the top wards bravely watched as they passed the windows, but bedclothes provided scant protection! The tube shelters were more crowded than ever, their bunks only being dismantled at the end of April. Although throughout the spring, Russian and allied forces advanced towards Berlin, people were very tired and food queues were longer.

All, however, was not alarm and despondency. There was much talk of social reconstruction and, in early March, almoners met with Sir William Beveridge. The Butler Education Act had come into force, and on the not-too-distant horizon stood the vision of a National Health Service, free and available to all from cradle to grave. Plans to rebuild city centres and move populations to new satellite towns were already in hand. Rapid developments in medical research were to bring about major changes. No longer would tuberculosis require lengthy sanatorium treatment, although almoners were still gowned and masked on the admission wards. A unit for the treatment of dysfunction in the thyroid and thymus glands produced one of the earliest colour films. Penicillin was revolutionising the treatment of infections, and there was growing concern for the treatment of the elderly soon to deserve its own speciality. On the 8th May, peace in Europe was declared and the years of blackout and sleepless nights were over.

Of the work of the almoner in this eventful year, my experience was of two London County Council hospitals, one in NW London and the other in SE London where I was an uncertified assistant almoner awaiting the full Institute training in 1947 on completion of my university extramural course. Fifty years ago patient stay was usually a matter of weeks or months and it was expected that every patient would have an initial interview. To some members of the medical and nursing staff, this was accepted as a necessity to ensure the cost of treatment would be met, but some redress in priorities was noted when a particularly autocratic ward sister reprimanded a patient: "This is not just a H.S.A. lady but a proper almoner." Each welfare area had its own assessment and collection departments so that further intervention in money matters was seldom needed. Provision of surgical appliances, out-patient treatment, convalescence and straightforward routine tasks were dealt with by clerical assistants.

Although the emphasis may have been different, social work with patients faced the same problems as it does now. Then bereavement included men and women killed as a result of enemy action; the loss of limbs and sight; of home and lifelong possessions. Long absences of husbands and fathers and of children evacuated for years made for difficulties in picking up the threads of family life. For the old and destitute, the forbidding workhouse, now renamed an institution, was the ultimate dread. In February, the "chronic sick" patients evacuated to a Base Hospital in the Midlands returned. As they had been nursed in bed with little rehabilitation, many had succumbed to pneumonia, but a mammoth effort had been made during these years to rescue a patient in her early 60s suffering from rheumatoid arthritis by six monthly applications to subscribers to the Royal Hospital and Home at Putney. Letters were delivered on foot and bicycle by staff at weekends all over London. At the end of two and a half years she had secured enough votes to be elected to a vacancy. In the excitement of preparing for this move, she had a heart attack and died. In May three Channel Islanders were admitted suffering from malnutrition. Their stories made everyone realise how acute their suffering had been. Poverty is remembered as being less of a problem. Uniform food rations, restaurant meals not exceeding 5/- (25p) together with furnished rents of 7/6 (40p) limited expenditure. National Assistance Officers had a more flexible approach especially to air raid victims and voluntary organisations such as SSAFA, FWA and the ICCA were ready to help.

In July came the General Election and the victory of the Labour Party under Clement Attlee – and in August atom bombs on Japan ended the war in the Far East. A diary entry for 8th October, "Antenatal Clinic so heavily booked it lasted from 9.30am to 3.30pm with no lunch break!" was surely a clear sign that peace had returned.

London 1995

ANOTHER FIELD –
THE INTRODUCTION OF THE ALMONER
TO GENERAL MEDICAL PRACTICE

Jane E. Paterson

There is little doubt that the credit for the introduction of the almoner to general medical practice must rest with the late Professor Frank Crew who, at the end of the Second World War, was appointed to the Chair of Public Health and Social Medicine at the University of Edinburgh. Shortly after taking up this post he must have had the chance to observe the work done by hospital almoners, and it was not long before he declared that the skills of the almoner were *"an instrument uniquely designed to fit the enquiring hand of Social Medicine"*. He decided to invite an almoner to join his staff, and in the autumn of 1947 I was appointed as a Departmental Assistant in Public Health and Social Medicine.

I came to this post after over eight years of hospital experience in both Scotland and England. I was to work under the supervision of one of the Department's senior members of staff, Dr Richard Scott. His background, prior to service in His Majesty's Forces, was that of general medical practice. Our task was to find a permanent population on which the Department could carry out studies appropriate to social medicine.

We decided to start our search for this population by offering health overhauls to the family members of all children admitted to one ward of the Royal Hospital for Sick Children over a certain period of time. This was followed by a study of married students, whose head – husband or father – was undertaking a university course or degree following discharge from HM Forces. However, it did not take us long to realise that these two groups could not be considered permanent, as on discharge the children could go home to other areas and the students would be likely to move out of Edinburgh on completion of their studies.

By the spring 1948 the National Health Service was about to be inaugurated, and this was bound to have an effect on four institutions in Edinburgh. These were the Public Dispensaries which provided free medical care for people not insured under the National Insurance Act of 1911, that is elderly people and the wives and children of insured workers. They also provided a valuable experience for medical students who could carry out "Dispensary Practice" as part of their studies. Two of these dispensaries decided to close when the National Health Service came into being; a third wished to continue its work of preparing students to work in medical missions, as it was a religious body; the fourth had gone so far as to compile a list of the names and addresses of patients who wished to continue with the dispensary in the event of a general practitioner being appointed under the new NHS.

Professor Crew was quick to spot the potential of this development; so it was that on 4 July 1948, Dr Scott and I were occupied in the task of transferring the names and addresses of our future "permanent population" to a card index in preparation for the events of the following day.

I suppose it was inevitable that, working in one of the poorer areas of the city, where one did not have to *search* for social problems, our first consideration was to give a service. Our academic obligations had to be fulfilled also, and right from the start we offered experience of working in the community to medical students, leaving the development of research and the teaching of social work students to a later stage.

It always amused me when hospital almoner colleagues used to enquire when I would be "returning to the field" as I was daily immersed in such things as acute illness, chronic illness, terminal illness, addiction, domestic violence, illegitimate pregnancy, poor housing, financial problems, all at an earlier stage than one might encounter them in hospital practice. Indeed, one lady almoner could never understand what I found to do, when I had "no beds". I wish I could have quoted to those doubting Thomases a remark made at a much later date by one of my medical colleagues that, "in general practice", one had a bed in every patient's house.

By the time we had secured our "permanent population", Dr Scott had become the first Professor of General Practice in the world, and the work had changed, with research and teaching being given high priority as Professor Crew had originally intended.

This, however, is anticipating events somewhat.

In the early 1950s Dr Scott published an article describing the work of the Unit, as it was called in those days, which attracted the attention of the Rockefeller Foundation, in New York. Dr Scott was invited to visit the USA to observe the work of the various institutions which had embarked on the teaching of medical students about the social component of medical care.

Before long the foundation had agreed to support an extension of the Unit, and about the same time the other dispensary agreed to join forces with us, bringing with them their staff and premises. So by 1955 there were two medical teams, each consisting of two or three doctors, one nurse and one medical social worker.

Realising that I would have to brush up my own professional knowledge, which had not kept pace with the times, I decided to visit the USA and I was granted a Rockefeller Fellowship to enable me to be "refreshed". On the advice of various American medical social workers who had visited the Unit, I was enrolled as a mature student at Simmons College School of Social Work in Boston, where I spent a most rewarding year.

Returning to Edinburgh in 1956, I found that a number of GPs in the city and its environs had been recruited to accept medical students in their practices, first as observers and then as participants in their work, much as medical social work students are placed in the departments of medical social work. About the same time what had been a voluntary activity for the students was made compulsory.

The GPs with their respective students were organised into tutorial groups, which met on a weekly basis. A medical social worker was always present at these meetings and took part on the discussions about the students patients.

Gradually, involvement in teaching increased for the medical social workers so that eventually they were holding supervisory interviews with the medical students in the same way as they did with their own medical social worker students. This involvement continued until my retirement in 1980. A more rewarding use of social work skills would be hard to find.

Edinburgh 1995

TRAINING WITH THE INSTITUTE OF ALMONERS: 1958

Ann Loxley

The institute was then housed at 42 Bedford Square, WC1, in a higgledy-piggledy warren of narrow staircases and small rooms. The Director was Helen Rees, followed later that year by Jean Snelling. There were two full-time tutors for each intake of about 12 to 16 students. The staff were abreast of new developments in social casework, and in touch with social work education in the States. The students were all graduates, and in my year all women in their early- to mid-twenties. Some must have been self- or family-funded, and others had grants from the Ministry of Health allocated through the institute. I was totally dependent on my maintenance grant, which I think was £210 to last from March to December, the length of the course. A dovetailed course ran from September to April, so the output was between 24 and 32 students a year to a profession then numbering around 1100 almoners in the UK. Some others qualified from a course in Edinburgh, but at that time generic university courses had hardly begun.

Students were required to have related degrees in the social sciences or social administration, so the course at the institute was able to concentrate on professional education, with about two-thirds of our time spent in placement. From March to July we had two days at the institute and three days a week in placement in student units in London teaching hospitals. From September to December we were in block placements scattered across the teaching hospitals in the rest of the country. My first placement was at St Mary's, Paddington and my second at the Royal Victoria Infirmary, Newcastle. At teaching hospitals, professional education of all kinds was a recognised part of their responsibilities and in both I was one of a succession of students allocated to an experienced supervisor. The tutor visited once during the course of the placement.

The teaching at the institute had two main areas of content. One was the biological and psychological knowledge base of medical social work, and the other the knowledge and practice of social casework. Subsidiary themes were the context of practice, that is the secondary setting, the organisational and administrative characteristics of hospitals, and the professionalisation of medical social work. We were taught social casework by our tutors and supervisors, and through our relationships with them we implicitly and explicitly learnt what was expected of us as professionals. The medical input was the responsibility of visiting lecturers, most of whom were London consultants, so that we had a sequence of specialists, ranging from Winnicott for paediatrics to Lister for general medicine. The teaching in psychology and psychiatry was an exception, in that the whole sequence was taught by Anthony Storr. Given the seniority and calibre of many of these outside lecturers, the institute must have been regarded as having some prestige. Our course was completed by a series of visits of observation to establishments in and around London, covering work such as industrial rehabilitation, terminal care, and physical and mental handicap.

Some medical lecturers were more able than others to relate biological information to psycho-social issues, but the input was predominantly physiological, and the traditionally didactic lectures covered the normal functioning, common disorders and their treatment, of body systems divided according to the recognised medical specialisms; the sequence ranged from paediatrics to geriatrics via nervous diseases, orthopaedics and dermatology. This smattering of medical information, together with the medical dictionary and standard text we were recommended to buy, at least enabled us not to be nonplussed when faced with the terminology of ward rounds or medical notes. It gave us a starting point for further learning in placement about the diseases or handicaps of our own patients, and the implications of the symptoms and treatment for their physical, social and emotional functioning.

I doubt, however, that many of the lectures were specifically tailored to social work students. They were probably the introductory overview given to student nurses, but they served to provide us with an elementary common base of knowledge with the medical, nursing and paramedical professions, and through the consultant lecturers were introduced to the dominant jargon and culture of the setting in which we were to work. This was the effect if not the intention. There was overt teaching from institute tutors and placement supervisors about the implications and constraints of the secondary setting – it seemed to be unquestioned that we were training for work in hospitals. We learnt about hospital and ward etiquette, the hierarchies in the other professions, the use of medical notes, the issue of confidentiality. It was stressed that while the medical social worker was part of the hospital team of which the consultant was indubitably the head because he had primary responsibility for the patient, the almoner was also a social caseworker in her own right, and therefore not part of a subordinate or ancillary service to medicine. Working relationships with doctors and nurses were guided on the one hand by the unique contribution medical social work was expected to make through its perception of the patient as a whole person, and on the other by the recognition that our place in the team had to be earned, often on a personal basis, so that we were taught to go slowly and tactfully using a conciliatory rather than a challenging mode. Looking back, I recognise that it was very much an adaptation of the traditional female role for which we were being educated, and that we were partly armed for the associated frustrations and struggles by the professionalisation of medical social work, to which I shall refer later.

The second axis of the course was the teaching of social casework which was based firmly on the writing of Charlotte Towle, Florence Hollis and Helen Perlman. The knowledge base was therefore in practice wisdom and in Freudian and Ego Psychology which echoed Storr's teaching of Human Growth and Development. The emphasis was not on pathology but on coping resources. The teaching method was predominantly through tutorial group discussion and close analysis of detailed case studies of individuals facing problems in their psycho-social environment, which invariably included situations of illness, accident or handicap. This dual focus, echoed in placement discussions of our own cases, enabled us to absorb and integrate the medical and psychological teaching with the skills and knowledge of the social caseworker.

In these small group discussions the stress was on painstaking, systematic method, analysing Social Study, Diagnosis and Treatment, of the Person, Problem and Place. Relationship was emphasised as the primary tool at all stages, working with "feelings as facts", and offering emotional support in partialising problems and identifying and fostering coping capacities. Particularly in supervision we were led to greater self-awareness in relating to people facing pain and loss, grief and depression. The use of external resources was acknowledged but less highly regarded, and we came to see ourselves as caseworkers for whom mobilising material help was a necessary but lesser skill. This was no doubt one cause of the conflict often presented in our first jobs when our chief function in the expectations of doctors and nurses was to arrange speedy discharges.

In placement students were given small caseloads, and work was expected to be in-depth quite quickly. Initially cases might be arranging discharge or convalescence but practice teachers did not shrink from allocating us to patients with disabling or terminal conditions. Learning was through studying patients' records, interviewing both in hospital and in the patients' homes (contrary to popular misconception in both my placements a lot of work was done outside hospital, and I remember one supervisor was taken aback when I faithfully recorded a conversation about the price of oranges). Process recording, and subsequent analysis and future planning, was the main teaching method. Each placement involved writing up a major case-study, which included accounts not only of work done with the patient and with other staff but discussion and explanation of the physical condition and of the social casework rationale. The two case-studies provided the material for assessment, for there were no examinations. The institute was rigorous and, as I remember, out of the cohort of about 12 at least two students were referred for further work, and another was advised to withdraw.

Although the training course was aimed exclusively at producing medical social caseworkers, we were told that almoners were related to probation and child care officers, and caseworkers to group and community workers, but we were not introduced to any of our relations. The socialisation was intense to our own profession. We learnt about its history and current organisation – even its salary scales and pension prospects, neither very lucrative; about its different committees, and its journal, the monthly "Almoner", which had high quality professional articles, and a regular births, marriages and deaths column, for the profession was small enough for this to have some meaning.

As I said above, we were imbued almost with a sense of mission about the social work contribution in humanising institutions which still trailed remnants of their Poor Law origins, and with a sense of professional self-respect, but we also learnt that we had to earn our acceptance. Almoners' work therefore had to be of a standard above reproach, so "professional" was equated with competence and commitment. We were unashamedly élitist, before that became a derogatory word. Selection was careful and searching; education and training were in the hands of women who themselves had this strong professional ethos, and the expectation was that students were being equipped to join a select group with a keen sense of its own tradition.

In some part this may have been due to the need to equip medical social workers with enough defences to cope in an often indifferent, sometimes hostile working environment. It may also have owed something to the grammar school tradition from which most of us came, and to the fight that intelligent middle class women had had to equip themselves with professional skills and academically valid knowledge, the fight which had also been that of social work as a profession.

Sadly, maybe what the institute taught in the post-war years until it ended in 1970 ultimately did a disservice to the needs of patients and to the contribution social work can make to health care. Perhaps skills which were sufficient when influence but not power was realisable, and high standards which sometimes led to a somewhat naïve idealism together, through the infighting between 1968 and 1970, and then in the division of spoils of 1974, unwittingly betrayed medical social work to the marginal position into which it is now in danger of declining.

Middlesex 1984

SOCIAL WORK SKILLS, ASSESSMENT AND CARE MANAGEMENT: 1995

Jacquin Northcott

This centenary year of health-related social work is an appropriate time to reflect on the continuing relevance of social work skills. Assessment and care management are not straightforward, but at a time of severe financial constraints it is tempting to try to fit a client into a preconceived "category of need", then take their seeming refusal for help at face value, and "zip up our purses" in relief.

Mr and Mrs P illustrate how important it is to find an effective and acceptable way of helping, as it would have been damaging and expensive if Mrs P had had to go into respite care as an emergency.

Mr P (82) had high blood pressure and a collapsed lung and had cared for his elderly wife for 10 years as she had chronic obstructive airways disease, emphysema, diabetes, arthritis and Alzheimer's disease. The only help he had accepted was occupational therapy adaptations and cleaning. However, he had now come to social services in crisis as his wife had fallen out of her chair and he could not lift her. After an emergency visit our OT referred them for possible personal, day and/or respite care.

Mr P greeted me with hostility – "No one has helped me, and if I could no longer manage social services would have to do something". I could have pointed out the help the OTs and home carer had given him, and how he had always refused other help in the past, but it was crucial to listen and understand the psychological factors – his projection of anger onto social services, his ambivalence at caring for his wife, his despair at the loss of his wife's companionship, his desperation for someone to care for him, his need to trust that someone could understand how locked in he was by the situation, his fear of change, and his fear of death.

Mr P was resistant to any suggestion of help and his wife repeated, "I only want my husband to look after me". The breakthrough came when I observed that I thought it was important that we took things slowly and there was no rush. He replied, "Yes that's it, you really understand". He visibly relaxed, as though the threat of sudden upheaval had receded. The practical outcome of this first interview was that we all three identified something that could possibly help – the home carer who came to clean could perhaps wash Mrs P's hair. Mrs P thought it nice to have a woman to wash her hair.

Mr and Mrs P greeted me warmly when I arrived for my second

interview. He first asked me to deliver his chiropody form, which I agreed to do as I felt it important for him to feel I understood his need for care. He then told me of his wife's hair-wash. At first she had not liked it but had accepted it happily when he insisted, and she confirmed this with me. After this Mr P talked of himself as in a trap with his wife's care. We both acknowledged that he had allowed himself to get into this situation but that I was a possible way out in that he could accept help gradually. The practical outcome of this second interview was that we agreed I should explore his wife being given a weekly bath.

Mr and Mrs P greeted me with considerable warmth at our third interview. Mr P enquired about his chiropody form and was reassured by my positive response. The hair-washing was going well and Mr P had decided that he would like his wife to be bathed. He confirmed that he was feeling more relaxed and that he wanted to increase his wife's care from others slowly. He was, though, concerned that I continue to visit.

Ten days after this visit, Mrs P died suddenly, at home, with her husband present. We are now approaching the anniversary of her death and I have seen Mr P four times at planned interviews, the timing and spacing have been discussed between us at each visit. He says he feels secure knowing that I am there, as a "lifeline" to social services, but he has not called on me between interviews, and he is pleased with the way he has coped on his own. When we have met he has talked openly of his own eventual death and had said of himself "I am in the infancy of being single". As for his wife he had talked of the care he had given her over the years, that he was happy that he had done all he could for her, and that her death was the best possible for her in the circumstances. She died peacefully at home with him and this has brought inestimable benefit to Mr P in the way he has handled his grief and life on his own.

Mr and Mrs P needs illustrate the importance of listening sensitively to the underlying meaning of what the client is saying and going at his or her pace when assessing what might be of practical help. It is crucial to use social work skills and knowledge to understand in practice what anger signifies, how important ambivalence, loss, projection and fear are, and how difficult it is for people to face change, however adverse their circumstances appear to the outsider. The practical and psychological needs of the client interact and both need to be addressed. It is necessary to respect the client and the power of the relationship you develop with him or her.

Mr and Mrs P's experiences also illustrate some of the problems elderly people have to contend with, and when and how social work intervention can be of help. They show that the quality of the care management will flow from the quality of the assessment and that this is a continuing process. They exemplify the importance of being able to commission appropriate help and the need to work closely with other helpers. In the event, Mr and Mrs P were only able to accept what might seem like just a little help but it was a major step for them.

As a crisis was prevented both before and after Mrs P's death the experiences also exemplify how cost effective it is to be able to work in this way both in terms of social work time, seven hours in all, and in terms of community resources. Assessment has always been part of the social work task and it is important to view it in all its complexity. It is counter-productive to allow ourselves to become swamped by the processes of commissioning the cheapest care and assessing financial liability which can sometimes seem a priority in our "contract culture". Preventing a breakdown makes economic sense and social work skills are necessary to achieve this.

London 1995

One Hundred Years of Health-Related Social Work

BASW POLICY STATEMENT, JUNE 1991

Social Work in Health Settings

Published with the assistance of the BASW Trust

Social workers are essential not only to clients who are using the health service but to ensure that social services and social work departments carry their responsibilities for community care and children and families appropriately.

BASW is concerned to see that the importance of social workers in health settings is recognised and sufficient numbers employed to ensure that client's needs for a "seamless" service between health and social care are properly met. "Health settings" means a place managed by any branch of the health service, hospitals, GP practice, clinics, accident & emergency units, etc.

Care of disabled and ill people starts with health care. Diagnosis, prognosis and treatment of a health problem underpin the decisions that need to be made about a person's social care. The social and emotional response of individuals and their families to diagnosis, prognosis and treatment affect future physical, mental and social health. Social workers need to be integral members of health teams to ensure that individuals and their families have access to all the knowledge and all the services required for a healthy response to new situations.

Social workers in health care can bridge the gaps of under-standing and of action that occur between health and social services.

Social workers bring to health professions an understanding of the social impact of ill health not only on the affected individual but upon the person's family and wider social networks.

Social workers in health settings should be employed by social services/social work departments, recognising that some social workers in health settings may be funded by charities or GP practices. Being employed in social services/social work departments ensures that:–

- the interface between health and social service allows a smooth transition from health to social care;

- there is clear responsibility for assessing need and for planning and enduring continuing care of disabled people;

- children's needs are appropriately met in health settings and LA offers appropriate service to disabled children;

- the priorities for care set by LAs are properly understood by health professions sharing the care of clients;

- social workers are given professional supervision and support and are clearly accountable for their practice.

Social workers should be based with health teams and should be managed by someone working in a health setting. This manager should hold a professional social work qualification, be part of the policy making process of social services departments and of the management structure of the health setting. Such a structure is essential to

a)   give informed supervision and support to social workers in health settings

b)   ensure the service is managed to the benefit of both health and social services

c)   ensure the social worker understands the different knowledge and skill of each health profession so that appropriate skills can be used to the client's benefit

d)   social work can inform the policies and practices of health teams

e)   ensure the substantial resources of the health service are used to benefit clients.

Mental health services

BASWs policy is to promote community based mental health services and believes that such provision should be jointly managed by health and social services/social work departments. With this proviso in mind the above policies still appertain.

BASW POLICY STATEMENT, JULY 1995

Care in the Community

Prepared by the Scotland Committee
of the British Association of Social Workers (BASW)
for the guidance of the new local authorities

BASW's Principles on Care in the Community

BASW has outlined the general principles which underpin the association's approach to social work practice in the leaflet "Social Work and the New Councils". Some additional principles were adopted when the new community care arrangements were being planned. They reflect the experience of our members who work closely with persons suffering from mental illnesses, physical disabilities and older people as well as carers.

- Most disabled or older persons are able to make appropriate decisions about their own care. It is important that for those requiring assistance, any assessment respects their rights and that services offer choice appropriate to the needs of clients and carers.

- Not all persons with disabilities need social work help but vulnerable groups should be assessed and have social care plans drawn up by qualified social workers based in health settings and area based teams.

- Social workers have formal duties in relation to persons with mental illnesses. They should also be able to act as advocates for others who are unable to take responsibility for their own care.

- No profession or agency has the total responsibility for providing services to persons who are disabled but care services provided should be co-ordinated by professionally qualified social workers.

The Griffiths Reports recommended that community care should be needs based and not determined by bureaucracy or cash. The association agrees with this approach.

BASW's views on how "Care in the Community" is working in 1995

There have been many positive developments. Many local authorities can take credit for the progress that has been made in giving information, involving users in the planning of services and in developing inter-agency collaboration.

There are, however, a number of matters which concern this association:

- The purchaser/provider split in responsibilities has resulted in a widespread confusion about what is the professional responsibility of social workers and other professional groups.

- Social workers are increasingly required to become rationers of services at the expense of the advocacy work which is required for many persons who require their help.

- The demands of emergency work or providing care for persons with complex needs have resulted in a severe reduction in the level of service provided for persons deemed to be "low priority".

- Community services for many groups of mentally ill persons are shamefully under resourced.

BASW's views on what needs to be done now

BASW is currently pressing for the Government to take action on the following matters:

- Clearer guidance must be given on what constitutes "care management". Central government must acknowledge the widespread variation in practice that exists throughout the country. They should acknowledge that the split in "purchaser" and "provider" roles has resulted in the marginalisation of some services.

- BASW supports the establishment of national standards for community care services. This is necessary to ensure that provision is based on the needs of individuals rather than by local resource constraints.

- Local authorities should recognise the distinction between community care services and the mechanism of providing it. They should not allow market forces to dictate care provision.

- Time and energy of social workers are spent on managing health and social services boundaries in the context of hospital admissions and discharges. More-appropriate use should be made of professional skills.

- Higher priority must be given to the provision of services for those in the community with a mental health problem particularly in housing, health and social work.

What BASW wants the new councils to do

BASW urges the new councils to maintain the commitment which has already been given by many existing councils and to develop corporate strategies in this area. This association asks councils to press government to finance them adequately to provide a full range of services for some of the most vulnerable people in society. In addition, BASW asks them to give attention to the following points in drawing up Care in the Community programmes.

- Set standards of care which will improve the quality of life of all users of services.

- Introduce care management systems based on a needs-led approach and which facilitate client choice and supports carers.

- Ensure that care managers have the full range of professional skills, personal qualities and experience that the posts require.

- Enable social workers to undertake advocacy, counselling and rehabilitation work for persons in need.

- Give priority to ensuring that new inter-agency arrangements for community care are put in place particularly with health and housing services.

- Ensure the continued deployment of social workers in hospital settings where they have established a valuable role.

BASW will be pleased to co-operate with all councils on these matters.

Suggested further reading

1. Ahmad, B:
    Black Perspectives in Social Work, Venture Press,
    Birmingham, 1990

2. Badawi, M & Biamonte, B:
    Social Work Practices in Health Care, Woodhead Faulkner,
    Cambridge, 1990

3. Bamford, T:
    The Future of Social Work, Macmillan, London, 1990

4. Bell, E. Moberley:
    The Story of Hospital Almoners, Faber & Faber, London,
    1961

5. Brearley, J:
    Counselling and Social Work, Open University Press,
    Buckingham, 1995

6. Butrym, Z:
    Social Work in Medical Care, Routledge & Kegan Paul,
    London, 1967

7. Butrym, Z:
    The Nature of Social Work, Macmillan, London, 1976

8. Bywaters, P:
    Case Finding and Screening for Social Work in Acute
    General Hospitals, British Journal of Social Work, Vol 21 pp
    19-39, 1991

9. Cooper, J:
    The Creation of the British Personal Social Services,
    Heinemann Educational Books, London, 1983

10. Goldberg, E M & Neill, J:
    Social Work in General Practice, George Allen & Unwin,
    London, 1972

11. Jones, K:
    Mental Health & Social Policy 1845-1959, Routledge & Kegan Paul, London, 1960

12. Timms, N:
    Psychiatric Social Work in Great Britain (1939-1962), Routledge & Kegan Paul, London, 1964

13. Walton, R W:
    Women in Social Work, Routledge & Kegan Paul, London, 1975

14. Younghusband, E L:
    Social Work in Britain: 1950-1975, George Allen & Unwin, London, 1978